The Agony of Polemos

La Agonía De Polemos

THE AGONY OF

POLEMOS

—CARLOS VIDELA—

Translated by Giammarco Simonelli

ANTELOPE HILL PUBLISHING

TABLE OF CONTENTS

PREFACE TO THE 2021 EDITION

A new edition of *The Agony of Polemos*, four years after it was initially written, deserves a careful revision. This new edition has been arranged emphasizing the ontological aspect of Polemos, a concept which was reclaimed principally by Heidegger from the Hellenic past. This, because the philosophy of the German thinker has been gaining renewed importance in recent years, is the foundation for a philosophical meditation focused on confronting the political and cultural hegemony of what is known as globalism.

The political area known as the "third position" or "national-populism," which encompasses different political entities that appeared in different periods and continents, has been especially receptive to this Heideggerian renewal. In fact, the greatest political theories have always emerged from deep meditation, embracing many more aspects than just the mere politics. Both the one known as "first political theory," that is, liberalism, and the "second theory," Marxism, as well as the "third political theory" of the nationalist movements, have all had true worldviews or ways of seeing the world and the nature of man as the basis for their political unfolding.

Among these, the third political theory is the most recent one. It arose as a revolutionary reaction against liberalism and the threat of Marxism, the latter a theory that was about fifty years ahead of the nationalist movements when these burst into the world's political scene at the beginning of the twentieth century. It can be said that the precursors of the third political theory date back to the eighteenth century, and the genealogy of these ideas in their modern shape is well detailed by Sternhell in *The Anti-Enlightenment Tradition*. However, a more convincing political philosophy of such theory came during the first decades of the last century. This process was not coordinated; rather it burst spontaneously into different countries and at different times. German, French, and Italian thinkers were the most important in Europe. However, after the defeat of nationalism during the Second World War, national populist thought acquired the greatest depth in the Americas, and especially in Argentina.

Many philosophical systems and thinkers served as the grounding of the third political theory. Some theories of Aristotle and his medieval Christian interpreters, which covered communitarianism and the political nature of man, were essential in this process. Much was also borrowed from Hegel and his theory of the embodiment of the Absolute in the state. Fichte's idealism was another essential piece, especially his *Addresses to the German Nation*, as well as that of Herder and his reclamation of the people (*völk*) as a historical subject. Nietzsche likewise was of great influence with his *Will to Power* and the heroic vision of life.

Nevertheless, it appears evident that the two exponents whose political philosophies reached the greatest insight in the field were Martin Heidegger and Giovanni Gentile. Between their ideas, Heideggerian ontology is the one which acquired the greatest importance for the refinement of a firmly grounded political project.

Aristotle, Hegel, and Nietzsche have been utilized by nearly every political current; however, Heidegger and Gentile are far more difficult to employ. It is certain that the Italian theorized about a societal structure that could encompass more than just nationalism, and that the German's philosophy has served as an inspiration for thinkers outside the nationalist realm, such as Sartre or Derrida. But with Heidegger, something is needed which must go beyond the mere intention of reclaiming certain aspects of his philosophy while leaving aside others. As the years pass on, his most political writings are becoming widely disseminated again. This delay has not been the consequence of ill-intentioned actions of the past; rather, the explanation is that immediately after the war, Heidegger's thought of the thirties and forties was lost, and even the philosopher himself did not bother to deal with this situation. Part of this nationalist ontology came to light during the eighties, only to return again at the center of various controversies which were sparked by the ambiguity of the various bibliographical references.

Today the scenario is different, as all of Heidegger's seminars given at the time of nationalist hegemony in Germany and Europe have been recovered and published, including his legendary *Black Notebooks*. There is now no doubt. Heidegger's ontology was connected to a way of thinking which considered of great importance a kind of nationalism, sovereignism, or identitarianism, whose roots had to be mainly popular or social. Also, most importantly, the foundation for this ontology is found in the concept of Polemos, translated by Heidegger as "confrontation." From this an ontology or study of Being originated in which the identitarian aspect was fundamental.

Having said this, it is clear that Heidegger's polemology has come to present itself as an authentic and radical philosophical principle in the domain of the third political theory.

Heidegger's Polemos lays the foundations for a new ethic rooted in the heroic vision of pre-capitalist societies. From these foundations emerges a new—yet, ancient—way of understanding man and communities, a collection of ideas and values through which Heidegger tried to oppose the liberal plan of his times, and with which the hegemony of contemporary globalism could likewise be opposed.

Carlos Videla

POLEMOLOGY

Polemos is a philosophical concept stemming from Greek culture that is reminiscent of a tradition and a way of understanding existence as old as mankind.

This natural principle—which was subsequently made culture—has been interpreted in the following complementary ways in different disciplines: ontologically as the experience of existence as confrontation, anthropologically as the struggle for life, and sociologically as the basis of heroic and agonal societies. Understanding and experiencing existence "polemologically" was preserved in the majority of known cultures until the appearance of the European liberal system of values. The replacement of the hero with the merchant and of traditional communities with consumer societies have essentially meant the dissolution of this ancestral way of seeing the world.

In this process, the deviation of the concept of freedom, essential to liberalism, has played an important role in the ontological subversion of the agonal tradition. Freedom, defined for millennia as the sovereign ability to determine personal and community boundaries, generating diversity and identity, has been transformed during the last centuries into precisely the opposite; that is, into the absence of limits.

Freedom was fundamental in the Greek *paideia*, the educational system based on the virtue of self-control and its extension into the autonomy of the *polis*. This virtue allowed for the making of autonomous decisions based on thoughtful judgments, with the limitations that community involvement entailed. Classical freedom, therefore, was based on discipline, rigor, control, and limit.

Liberalism, born in the sixteenth century, rebelled against this tradition, even though during its first centuries of existence it kept some ties with classical culture. During this period, authors such as John Locke were dynamiting the foundations of the traditional culture by defining the concept of self-control as something irrational, pre-modern, paternalistic, and even tyrannical. The liberal order's idea of freedom was based on emancipation from the restraints of tradition, social and economic rules, and even from the limits of nature. Locke, the first philosopher of liberalism, considered freedom as the individual ability to think, stripped of any cultural or communitarian ties. Even belonging to a family, a community, or a nation had to be something thought out by the individual will and accepted or rejected following a personal and detached consideration. Broader views were discarded or put aside as secondary. On this premise, Hobbes stipulated that human beings were autonomous, unconnected, and therefore freedom itself was achieved *where law was silenced*, and where norms—*nomos*—and customs and community ties were reduced to a minimum.

The ancient individual choice based on self-control and the limits imposed by social integrity, culture, and connection to nature was turned into a decision driven by selfishness and devoid of any ethical boundary over individual reason. Man, who once was the political animal of the *paideia* and classical virtue, gave way to the liberal individualist.

This concept of freedom without limits generated a new cultural principle that pervaded the social, economic, and political domains over the following centuries. In this transformation, productive labor has drifted into a deregulated and transnational financial capitalism, a libertarian and right-wing anarcho-capitalism with deeply negative effects on human nature. Furthermore, this process has cleared the way for a nihilistic culture, promoted by the new progressive and transhumanist left, in which the lack of identity reigns at a personal and communal level.

The globalist world order of our days derives directly from the interpretation of freedom as a radical opposition to the pre-modern virtue of self-control. Globalism is the implementation on a planetary scale of a culture based on the end of the concept of limit, a plan for a society based on universality and undifferentiation.

Any philosophical and political project that truly intends to confront the current system must base its worldview on aspects that invalidate the conceptual basis of liberalism. As such, the ideas that are radically antagonistic to global liberalism are represented by diversity, particularity, identity, and limits. Neither proletarian universalism nor deconstructive progressivism could and will ever be able to stand up to present-day globalism. Therefore, the alleged omnipotence of postmodernism and deconstructionism is not such, and for this reason they have been neutralized and assimilated into the hegemonic globalist bloc since the last several decades.

The background to this situation lies in the philosophical roots shared by liberalism and the so-called "cultural Marxism." Postmodern authors attempted to use precisely the concepts of undifferentiation, abstraction, deterritorialization, and desubjectification for their revolutionary project, which only reinforced the absence of limits implied in the liberal project. These thinkers did not understand that the foundation of the liberal-capitalist system was not the same as that of the pre-capitalist West and, eager to destroy economic liberalism, they focused their efforts on subverting the traditional culture, which had a bare connection, if any at all, to the mercantile system imposed during modernity. This misconception has made their revolutionary struggles mostly ineffective at weakening the core of their objectives: the global financial power of capitalism. The battles of progressivism, for example, became sooner or later financed by capitalist millionaires such as George Soros or Bill Gates, neutralizing in this way any hypothetical threat to the system. This did not happen as the result of some plan arranged by international finance, but simply because the relationship between philosophies ended up uniting currents of thought that had common objectives. There is nothing more beneficial to the globalist economic system than the deconstructed and boundary-less societies promoted by the new left. From this combination of interests and similarities the so-called "historical globalist bloc" was born, comprising a group of entities and schools of thought of which many can seem antagonistic at a glance, but which in reality have merged neoliberal capitalism and leftist progressivism.

HEIDEGGER'S POLEMOS

Identity and particularity have been important concepts in the political thought of the so-called nationalist ideological movement, that third political theory, the alternative to liberalism and to the by-products of Marxism. Great philosophers, especially from Germany and Italy, reached important heights in the development of a philosophical foundation that would overcome the cultural hegemony of liberal universalism in each area of influence. Perhaps the most outstanding thinker in this line was Martin Heidegger, with his radical theory on "Being as confrontation": on Polemos, a philosophy termed by Derrida as "philopolemology"[1] and as "polemology" by others.[2] Heidegger's Polemos represented a complete turning point in the spiritual development of modern man. Hence, it confronted the hegemony of the liberal plan that had been in development over the course of the last three hundred years.

Polemos (πόλεμος) is a term that was originally conceived by Heraclitus of Ephesus, a Greek thinker of the sixth century BC. Its most common meaning is struggle, conflict, or confrontation, but always understood in its ontological aspect. In the opinion of the Chilean philosopher Jorge Rivera,[3] Heraclitus was the first one that pondered on Being and the creator of a mythical-poetic perspective

---

[1] Derrida, "Heidegger's Ear."

[2] Heidegger's polemology is not to be confused with the sociological discipline bearing the same name, created by Gaston Bouthoul. Bouthoul's polemological studies are related to the demographic and biological purpose of war. This doctrine produced eponymous editorial publications, and led to the establishment of academies, mainly in France. Recently, Bouthoul's polemology has experienced a sort of resurgence and academic recognition.

[3] See Rivera, *Heráclito, El Esplendente* (only in Spanish).

that was starting to be adopted in theoretical thinking. Heraclitus was therefore the father of ontology or the study of Being; hence his constant dialogue with the German thinker, perhaps the greatest proponent of the Heraclitean view in modern philosophy.

According to Heraclitus, struggle allowed for things to exist instead of not existing, in such a way that struggle was the source of diversity in the world (*panta*). As the Greek thinker wrote in his famous fragment 53: "Polemos is the father of all and the king of all."[4] Starting from this and other fragments of Heraclitus' writings, Heidegger conducted his own radical polemological thought.

Whether the Heideggerian interpretation of Heraclitus was correct or not has been largely debated. This doubt will probably remain a matter of discussion for many decades, if it will ever be resolved at all. What is important now is that Heidegger achieved, through Heraclitus' inspiration, a profoundly radical philosophy, and that this opens the possibility to establish it as the system of values capable of opposing liberalism and its variants in the twenty-first century.

In the Heideggerian polemology of Heraclitean roots, men and beings in general shared one thing in common: they all existed, they all were beings. Therefore, Being was something common to all entities, the underlying foundation without which differentiation and ontological limit could not exist. Being (with a capital letter) was the universal quality and the wellspring of all that has existed, exists, and will exist. Heidegger, like many other philosophers, relentlessly sought the essence of existence; that which made being, instead of not being, possible. He found the answer in Polemos. To Heidegger, Being was not about the beings taken individually, nor the sum of all beings in a unified entity. Being was the ability to be different.

---

[4] Burnet, "Herakleitos of Ephesos," 136.

In the Heideggerian perspective, coming to be meant emerging from uniformity into a shape.[5] Being or existing meant for Heidegger to emerge, to acquire visibility and contrast. Consequently, all beings had in common the characteristic of having distinct boundaries, limits that made having an identity easier for them. Emerging from the "not-Being," or unified and undifferentiated Being, into tangible existence generated an identity which would inevitably dominate or clash with other identities. Heidegger believed that this was Polemos: an ontological conflict, and a new—or renewed—radical way of understanding man and the world.

Polemos—or confrontation, as Heidegger meant it—represented the fundamental principle of man and nature. Thus their essence *was* confrontation—confrontation when it comes to rising as individuals, families, clans, and the people of a nation; confrontation for long-term survival and preservation as perpetual entities; and confrontation when interpreting and understanding the world.

This radical ontology that understood the way of life or human existence—called by Heidegger "being-there," or *Dasein*, in German—as conflict, presented itself as a cultural foundation that was absolutely antithetical to the figure of the free and universal human being depicted by liberalism. Polemos as a way of being was a revolutionary idea that, if assimilated by the human spirit, would destroy the foundation of the current universalistic civilization, restoring the value of diversity, limits, and identity. The modern restoration of Polemos, therefore, presented itself firstly as a radical ontological foundation from which would then inevitably stem an alternative cultural project to liberalism. Heidegger himself acknowledged that

---

[5] Collin Cleary describes this in his article "Heidegger Against the Traditionalists" as follows: "During this time [the 1930s], Heidegger began utilizing *Seyn*, an archaic German spelling of *Sein* (Being). But why? What did this signify? It was not simply eccentricity on Heidegger's part. By *Seyn*, Heidegger meant something distinct from *Sein*, which refers to the Being that beings have ('Being as such'). *Seyn* instead refers to what Heidegger calls elsewhere 'the clearing' (*die Lichtung*). This metaphorical expression refers to a clearing in a forest, which allows light to enter in and illuminate what stands within the clearing. Thomas Sheehan describes Heidegger's clearing as 'the always already opened-up "space" that makes the being of things (phenomenologically: the intelligibility of things) possible and necessary.' The clearing is what 'gives' Being."

his polemology was so radical that even considering it revolutionary would be very a conservative claim.[6] Polemos, intended as Being or as the foundation of existential experience, was an idea that could not only cancel out the liberal project of the last three hundred years, but also bring down the cultural foundation built in the West since the "oblivion of Being" which had occurred. According to Heidegger and a rich tradition of thinkers, this oblivion began with Plato's metaphysics onwards.

As the American professor Gregory Fried claimed, Heidegger's Polemos encompassed the entire problem of the conflict between nationalism and ideological globalism, and the debate between the sense of belonging and exclusion, and between particularity and universalism.[7] Polemos, therefore, was the most radical conception to set against the liberal system, certainly much more than the "radicalization" of postmodernism, as pointed out by Fried when evaluating the new left of the twenty-first century and its plan of deconstruction, which, as it has been argued, ended up consolidating the globalist order. Stated Fried:

> I shall argue that their radicalization of the assault on modernism,[8] the liberal regime, and the Enlightenment only aggravates the dangers facing us. The postmodernists often fail to realize how much more radical are both Heidegger and Nietzsche than they.[9]

Polemos was undoubtedly the cornerstone of Heideggerian philosophy in the thirties and forties, a key historical moment for Germany and the world. With the help of Polemos, Heidegger constructed a political philosophy that has come to light only in recent years. For example, the text of *Nature, History, State*, his most openly nationalistic seminar, along with *On Hegel's Philosophy of Right*, was discovered by coincidence in 1999, finally published in German in 2009, and printed in Spanish only in 2018. So too happened with the

---

[6] See Heidegger, *Ponderings VII-XI*.
[7] See Fried, *Heidegger's Polemos*.
[8] That is, postmodern subversion.
[9] Fried, *Heidegger's Polemos*, 14.

Black Notebooks, Heidegger's intimate writings, dating from 1931 to the sixties. To date, only his notes that date back to 1941 have been published, but they have been sufficient to trigger a wave of controversies over his political orientation. Undoubtedly, Heideggerian nationalism and its involvement with National Socialism will keep sparking both new and renovated controversies in the decades to come, while the study of his philopolemology will allow for the laying out of a more insightful philosophical foundation, useful to identitarian political projects.

POLEMOLOGICAL ONTOLOGY

Heidegger's Polemos was a philosophical intuition that came early in the German thinker's life. However, it would not take its true form until the early 1930s. Fried saw traces of polemological ontology in *Being and Time*, dated 1927, despite the fact that Heidegger himself repeatedly admitted that his magnum opus was an unsuccessful attempt at establishing his true philosophy. It is of common knowledge that as the Weimar Republic entered in a spiral of decadence, to collapse later on with the National Socialist seizure of power, Heidegger's polemological thought began to take an increasingly clearer shape. Because of this, one could speculate that Heidegger's early involvement in National Socialism[10] was linked to the development of his polemological ontology. If so, it would not be surprising if he saw in National Socialism the arrival of the spirit of Polemos on German soil, in the same way as the great psychiatrist Carl Jung saw in these events the return of the ancient Germanic god Wotan.

In 1933 Heidegger announced to Carl Schmitt that his studies on Heraclitus had provided him a new ontological conception of conflict. The following year he made his studies on Polemos publicly known for the first time in the course on the German poet Hölderlin, which coincided with a re-evaluation of his philosophy called the

---

[10] The *Black Notebooks* have proved that Heidegger adhered to National Socialism as early as 1930.

"turn" (*kehre*).[11] At that time, he still called this philosophical principle "struggle" (*kampf*) or "strife" (*streit*), replacing it later with
"confrontation" (*ausereinandersetzung*). Struggle, dispute, and confrontation will be always similar principles in Heideggerian polemology. By the time of his seminar on Hegel in 1934 and the one in
1935, later published as *Introduction to Metaphysics*, confrontation
was already clearly the Polemos of Heraclitus:

> The word *polemos* with which the fragment begins does not
> mean "war" [*Krieg*], but rather what is meant by the word *eris*,
> which Heraclitus uses in the same sense. But this means
> "strife" [*Streit*]—but strife not as quarrel and squabble and
> mere discord, and most certainly not the violent treatment
> and repression of the opponent—but rather an Aus-einander-
> setzung of a kind in which the essence of those who step out
> against each other in con-frontation [*die sich aus-einander-
> setzen*] exposes itself to the other [*sich aussetzt dem anderen*]
> and thus shows itself and comes into appearance, that is, in a
> Greek sense, into what is unconcealed and true.[12]

Later on, Heideggerian polemology would unfold in other seminars
such as the aforementioned *Nature, History, State* in 1933–34, *Logic
as the Question Concerning the Essence of Language* in 1934, *On Hegel's Philosophy of Right* in 1934–35, *The Origin of the Work of Art* in
1935–36, *Contributions to Philosophy* in 1936–38, the seminars on
Nietzsche in the late thirties, the ones on Hölderlin in the early forties, the one on *Parmenides* in 1942–43 and the first two seminars
on Heraclitus in 1944, which denote a philosophy with markedly political overtones, where the determination to form peoples with a
historical destiny, the importance of the leader and of the state, the

---

[11] "The much-discussed Kehre, the so-called turn in Heidegger's thought, must be
understood in terms of polemos as well. This turn is often treated as a decisive
'second sailing' in Heidegger's own thought away from the subjectivist leanings of
the analytic of Dasein along a more solidly antimetaphysical path." (Fried,
Heidegger's Polemos, 16.)

[12] Fried, *Heidegger's Polemos*, 37.

popular elites, and the answer to the question of "the One" as an authentic identity in front of the Other, all acquired great depth.

CONFRONTATION

Polemos was a concept that referred to the rise of beings as differentiated entities. It also implied the struggle for the preservation of this difference. Lastly, it meant a way of being, of existing, a way of living in the world as human beings capable of interpreting reality:

> [S]truggle is the *innermost necessity* of beings as a whole.... beings come to Being through struggle.... For struggle proves to be setting things into Being and holding them there, by making them emerge yet holding them fast.... the essence of Being is struggle; every Being passes through decision, victory and defeat.[13]

According to the Heideggerian analysis, the Heraclitean term *panta*, meaning the diversity of beings, would reveal itself because of Polemos, the confrontation. It was Polemos who forced the unified Being to differentiate and manifest itself in its plural character. According to Heraclitus, it was Polemos who set off confrontation within the stillness of the One, "obliging" this undifferentiated nothingness to take on a multiplicity of shapes, each one facing off the other in order to obtain its own identity. In the absence of conflict everything melted into a stable nothingness, motionless and unchanging, lacking struggle and without a shape. Heraclitus believed that the prerequisite for things to exist and for the world to be experienced, in its differentiated and diverse aspect, was existence in conflict, in the confrontation that allowed two different entities to position

---

[13] Heidegger, *On the Essence of Truth*, 74–75.

themselves facing each other. Starting from a tiny insect or inanimate entity up to man, nations, and cultures, everything that could be recognized or named as something distinct was a child of Polemos.[14]

Fried gives an account of how the word confrontation (*Auseinandersetzung*), in German, has its root in the concepts of a setting or positioning (*Setzung*) out and apart (*aus*) from another entity (*einander*). So, confrontation is "a laying out and setting forth that establishes and differentiates" in which "sides distinguish themselves from one another and take up positions confronting one another, in everything from respectful, vigorous debate to trench warfare."[15] Polemos or confrontation (*Auseinandersetzung*) was an ontological concept that described the way in which beings emerged, came into being, and how they related to each other.

> Polemos does not mean "war" (*Krieg*) in the sense of "battle" (*Schlacht*), not even "fight" (*Kampf*), but rather "decision" (*Entscheidung*); that is "confrontation" (*Auseinandersetzung*), "decision" (*Ent-scheidung*): to let emerge from separation, to let appear in natural contrast—to let the differences of the beings rise. . . . This is the same: Logos, Pyr, Eris, Polemos.[16]

According to Heidegger, in the heroic world view of the Greeks the existential experience was governed by the *logos,* which was a way of experiencing the world polemologically, among diversity and boundaries. The *logos* was a light, a guide amidst the darkness of the void, of what is shapeless and without appearance. Heidegger gave a meaning to the word *logos* that was related to the ability to bring together that which is dispersed or undifferentiated so that a particular being could emerge. Without the *logos* the world would lose its

---

[14] Perhaps, the etymology of the word "exist" should be taken into consideration: "'to have actual being of any kind, actually be at a certain moment or throughout a certain period of time,' c. 1600, from French *exister* (17c.), from Latin *existere/exsistere* 'to step out, stand forth, emerge, appear; exist, be'" (via Online Etymology Dictionary).

[15] Fried, *Heidegger's Polemos*, 15.

[16] Heidegger, *Anmerkungen I–V*. Translated by Giammarco Simonelli.

organization and the logic established by the reunion of what was once dispersed, transforming itself again into something chaotic, unintelligible, and without any point of reference for its assimilation.[17] Therefore, Polemos, conflict, did not destroy things but, on the contrary, it preserved unity by differentiating, by rendering the diverse entities of the world perceivable as distinct. "Confrontation does not divide unity, much less destroy it. It builds unity; it is the gathering (*logos*). *Polemos* and *logos* are the same."[18]

But conflict did not only allow for diversity and, consequently, the rise or birth of the variety of shapes of the world. Other than being the "father of all things," conflict was also that which made the preservation of all beings possible. Conflict, as stated by Heraclitus, was Father and King of all things, because the primordial struggle made it possible to overcome the countless obstacles to existence, guaranteeing preservation. "War [Polemos] is the father [*Pater*] of all and the king [*Basileus*] of all [*panta*]; and some he has made gods and some men, some bond and some free."[19] In line with Heideggerian polemology, the absence of conflict would prevent the various forms and shapes of the beings from emerging, and, without the ability to fight, they would not be able to preserve themselves either. Without Polemos, without the sacrifice of the original partition,[20] the multiple would unify again. In the absence of confrontation, things would disappear, and the world would fall into an indeterminate state.

Heidegger argued that experiencing the world in its unified aspect was called *Hen* by Heraclitus. What unified it was the lightning,

---

[17] In the seminars on Heraclitus in 1943 and 1944, Heidegger mentions two types of logos, the Logos with the capital letter which refers to the Being in its unified character, and the *logos* with a lower case which indicates the human ability to bring together or unify in order to organize and experience the world and the diversity of beings. (Heidegger, *Heraclitus*).

[18] Heidegger, *Introduction to Metaphysics*, 65.

[19] Burnet, "Herakleitos of Ephesos," 136.

[20] Sacrifice, in its ritual and mythological meaning, referred to the division of the original unified being, which was dismembered, thus originating the diversity of entities. Several examples are the division of *Purusha* in the Vedic tradition, Ymir in the Germanic tradition, the Brown Bull of Cooley for the Celts, and the sacrifice of Atlas in Greek mythology.

Keranos, the blinding light which dissolved shapes and identities. It allowed the experience of existence in a symmetrical and egalitarian way, with no differences or limits. This was the unified experience of the entities, a necessary one since "experiencing the Being" in its entirety allowed the coming into contact with the source from which difference emanates, the origin and unification of all that existed, exists, and will exist. Nevertheless, this experience had to come "out of" diversity, otherwise it could not be experienced. Only those beings differentiated through Polemos could venture and experience what Being could be, otherwise they would remain immersed, unified, and diluted in that primordial unity, without the possibility of "distancing" themselves in order to witness it from the outside.

This is an important point because polemology did not establish a dualism between the Being and man but rather the contrary: it established a much deeper connection between these two, reaching deeper than where the contemporary "oblivion of Being" managed to. In fact, the lack of difference and ontological confrontation of modernity has in no case lead to experiencing the Being in its unified character; instead, contemporary culture has led to the absence of any existential experience, to the lack of a particular way of being that allows us to listen to the voice of Being or Polemos.

POLIS AND POLEMOS

In order to be in the world without being diluted to "shapeless-ness," the human being, during his existential experience, had to remain constantly differentiated by his own identity, especially through the cultural identity of language, defined by Heidegger as "the house of Being." Thus, the human being existed in proportion with his understanding of the world and how it gave meaning to it, "appropriating" reality through the codes of a cultural identity. This appropriation was a permanent passage of meaning and, conse-quently, of differentiation; of a permanent Polemos or confrontation in order to "steal" a world, to create a "map of meaning," a "home-land" or *polis* at the expense of the undifferentiated. In accordance with this, the human being in Heideggerian polemology was the be-ing in its differentiated form, which experienced a world in order.

> As Heraclitus thinks it, struggle first and foremost allows what essentially unfolds to step apart in opposition, first allows po-sition and status and rank to establish themselves in coming to presence. . . . In confrontation, world comes to be.[21]

With the creation of "a world" the human being obtained a "truth,"[22] a space of cultural significance by means of what Heidegger de-scribed as a "disclosure," the act of bringing out of what is hidden

---

[21] Heidegger, *Introduction to Metaphysics*, 65.
[22] Heidegger rewrote the Greek term *aletheia*, which is commonly understood as "truth" and "disclosure." He wrote it with the prefix "a" separated *(a-letheia)* in order to emphasize the words *a* ("without"), and *lethe* ("concealment" or "oblivion").

and invisible and pushing the undifferentiated toward difference, always through confrontation. Truth, according to Heidegger, was not a metaphysical idea nor an everlasting substance, and hence it did not have an ethical meaning but an ontological one.

In Heidegger's philosophy, the polemological existential experience of the human being was always collective. Man stole from the undifferentiated Being a cultural interpretation of the world. Along these lines, the "earth"—a term which Heidegger used when referring to objects without meaning—acquired an interpretation that revealed those objects unveiled, free of concealment, bearers of a meaning, a truth. This Polemos was the product of an interpretation or hermeneutics based on communitarian codes—especially language, considered as the house of the collective being—that reached its highest expression, as Heidegger always emphasized, in the foundational disclosing of poets, intellectuals, and statesmen.

To illustrate this process of un-concealment of the foundational truth of the human being, one can observe the creation of cultures, traditions, and nations. For instance, the conquistadors who landed in America had to confront a territory that was for them devoid of any cultural meaning, an indistinct land to which they attributed a truth through their understanding or *logos* by naming and baptizing mountains, rivers, and valleys in the image of their own culture and identity. Gradually, out of the void a new world emerged, a new homeland or cultural foundation full of meanings that had to be defended materially and spiritually in order to be preserved. However, this process of creation never ends, but continues in every moment, although it is always defined by an original identity or fundamental truth, the "National Being." Therefore it is always alive, and must never be mummified by ideological conservatism because this becoming demands adaptation and a steadfast understanding of the world.

Without confrontation, without the preservation of the identitarian truth, the world would vanish and return to be a mere wasteland. Beings would be predetermined, flat, and transparent, just as modern science requires to see objects in their universal character, composed of matter and not as bearers of a meaning determined by man during his life experience.

The polemological interpretation of the human being was a strife between the "earth" and the "world," between chaos and nature, between the void and identity. For this reason, the light of truth had to be conquered, to be stolen from Being. "The opposition of world and earth is strife,"[23] as Heidegger stated in *The Origin of the Work of Art*—a struggle for the self-affirmation and the authenticity of human existence.

Truth was what transformed the meaningless earth into a world accessible to understanding, a cultural space or map that conveyed an identity to the life experience of the human being or *Dasein*, differentiating it from Being in its unified state. So, truth, "is the innermost Auseinandersetzung [confrontation] of the essence of the human with beings as a whole," in Fried's words.[24] This identity, however, never distanced *Dasein* from Being; on the contrary, it bound them more than anything in a perpetual polemological relation. For this reason, Fried explains that according to Heidegger:

> Being and *Dasein* belong together in Polemos. Polemos takes place *between* ourselves (Da-sein) and Being (Sein). Polemos is Da-Sein.... *Truth*, as *Unverborgenheit* (un-concealedness) and *a-lētheia*, is polemos. For Heidegger, truth understood ontologically is the opening up of a world, the making manifest of beings for Dasein's understanding of Being. But this opening up, this making manifest, is always a struggle to bring forth from concealedness, from *lēthē*. Indeed, for anything to be at issue is dependent on truth as Polemos.... For Heidegger, we *are* polemically; our Dasein *is* polemos.... In the temporal structure of its existence, Dasein engages in polemos.[25]

This polemological relation between the human being and his existential experience before the world was not, in Heidegger's view, the result of a dualistic confrontation between the subject and the object of the world, intended as the mere reflection of lifeless things (as

---

23 Heidegger, "The Origin of the Work of Art," 26.
24 Fried, *Heidegger's Polemos*, 58.
25 Fried, *Heidegger's Polemos*, 16–17.

established by the Cartesian dualism that made way for contemporary scientism), but it was represented as the "appropriation"—theft—of a world.

The Heideggerian interpretation of the confrontation between human experience and the sterile earth seems to be in line with the idealism of one of the first philosophers of nationalism, the German idealist Johann Gottlieb Fichte, as well as with the philosophy of Giovanni Gentile, the most important intellectual of Italian Fascism.

According to Fichte, the acting "I," that is, the subject in the act of understanding or knowing reality—which is always an "acting we," since interpretation requires a cultural base—acted on the external object, on an entity that represented an obstacle.[26] This obstacle, at first, prompted an inevitable confrontation, a conflict with the entity that was foreign to the subject which, despite generating conflict, also bonded them as opponents, because the object ceased to be simply an object, revealing itself united to the subject, but in opposition to it, transforming itself into an anti-subject, a negative subject. Conflict and difference then made way for a change in the subject, induced by the forced interpretation of what was being faced. So, the existential experience was a perpetual interpretative confrontation with the obstacles that came in the way. This eternal clash between subject and object caused by the activity of interpretation was always dynamic, a constant motion or continuous act. As Giovanni Gentile[27] remarked, the fire—the subject—would always be in need of new fuel—the confrontation with the world—in order to keep burning.[28]

---

[26] See Fichte, *Gesamtausgabe.* and Fichte, *Sammtliche Werke.*

[27] The philosophy of Gentile has been called "actual idealism."

[28] The Italian philosopher Diego Fusaro has pointed out that the idealism of Fichte and Gentile could be defined as a "polemological metaphysics," an "ontology of revolution," a "transcendental praxis," or a "philosophy of action." According to Fusaro, the current dualistic system in its knowledge of the world deems objects as presences (*vorhandenheit*), not as the idealism of Fichte and Gentile, or the Heideggerian confrontation (*gegenstand*), where these objects come to be part of the identity of the individual. The individual, in the societies of contemporary globalism, lacks the inner strength necessary for "the praxis of revolutionary action," that action which generates worlds and difference through appropriation. In Fusaro's words, the Not-I (the earth, in Heidegger's words) is currently presented as "pure independent objectivity," which leaves man incapable of taking action,

This polemological existential experience also conveyed a political interpretation of the relation between the peoples and of the clash of the different fundamental truths. The unconcealed truths generated an identity that irremediably confronted other identities. This confrontation did not necessarily imply violence; on the contrary, Heideggerian confrontation, as Fried notes, implied that one has to "take seriously the possibilities offered by the Other in a respectfully agonal encounter."[29] In this context, respect between peoples was based on an identitarian and independent attitude and on diversity, but at the same time it was also characterized by an "appropriating" manner when facing one another. The French intellectual Alain de Benoist stated that identity, or the truth of a people, always shakes when colliding with another. Confronting the Other leaves marks on the identity, and in response it can either consolidate its own traits or produce new ones. In fact, human groups are not conscious of their distinguishing elements until their characteristics in certain domains are compared—confronted—with the characteristics of other groups in those same domains. This is the only way to constitute degrees of comparison which bring out identitarian characteristics. No people or group can claim a characteristic, such as being good hunters, fighters, or traders, if there is no other group with which they can compare these skills.

The cultural and political implications of this polemological philosophy were not missed by Fried:

Embracing this sense of a productively confrontational conversation among peoples means rejecting an ideal of the liberal Enlightenment: global government or some kind of federated world order, and the Kantian vision of perpetual

---

deprived of the ability to generate the fire evoked by Gentile or by the Heideggerian Polemos. Thus, reality presents itself as exploitable, a sort of still life, in which objects are only suitable for consumption, a characteristic that transforms man into a spectator of lifeless objects, alienating him from the world in his individualistic subjectivity. Guy Debord referred to this type of culture as the "society of the spectacle," and not because of its access to entertainment but due to the condition of the subject as a spectator before a given world, placed before the subject with a predetermined and standardized meaning.

[29] Fried, *Heidegger's Polemos*, 18.

peace. Heidegger believes that polemos with Being must take place within the compass of a finite world: that of a historical community, a *Volk*. By confronting the trajectory of the givenness of its own history, a Volk simultaneously preserves its particularity and renews its history, while making possible a transformative conversation, that is, a polemos, with other peoples. This is what Heidegger had hoped for from the National Socialist revolution: the paradoxically transformative preservation of the community's form of life through polemos, against modernity's homogenizing and totalizing tendencies, which Heidegger designates broadly as Liberalism.[30]

---

[30] Ibid., 18–19.

ONTOLOGICAL NATIONALISM

Heidegger thought that the People was the community defined by a genuine way of being or communitarian *Dasein*, the bearer of a truth unconcealed through Polemos. In order to achieve this identity, the human group had to act with resolve, and had to share a language and, above all, a native land—an unconcealed territory— that would give to this people the possibility to thrive. Earth, transformed into a cultural world, had to be the spatial medium that enabled the genuine development of the way of being, of the truth of this people.

Heidegger believed that the identitarian existence of a nation relied on the three factors of nature, history, and state, as he explained in his seminar bearing the same name, held from late 1933 to early 1934.

But nature, history, and state were not merely a territory, a common history, and a state organization; instead, the German philosopher held that these principles were to be understood in an existential sense.

Nature, understood as man's existential experience, was for Heidegger the Heraclitean *physis*. This nature had the ability of disclosing beings, of development by means of a shift from concealedness and undifferentiation toward a differentiated way of being. Hence, nature or territory was the homeland out of which a way of being originated.

In the same way, history was related to a fundamental constitution of existence, a temporal experience, intrinsic to man. This was not based on a continuous present or "nows," as supposed by modern schools of thought, but it was related to a temporal experience

connected with the fundamental origin of the past and of the ances-
tors, together with the possibilities of the historical destiny of the
nation. Therefore, the existential time was a "just happened" and an
"about to happen." This experience of temporality made men beings
who had a way of living in a community with a historical background—historical *Dasein*—a definition that, for Heidegger, was not
related to living in a society, but it expressed a way of being in which
being human is "in a community, to carry in oneself the possibility
and the necessity of giving form to and fulfilling one's own Being and
the Being of the community."[31]

To give form and fulfillment to "one's own Being and the Being of
the community" was a status, a state or way of being. Regarding the
state of being of a people, it depended on its determination, which
embodied itself in a state. The state was therefore the historical fulfillment of a way of being unconcealed in *physis* and carried out by
the body of the state; that is, by the people as the constitutive entity
of a way of being. This was led by the statesman, the leader, the one
who "understands, considers, and brings about what people and
state are."[32]

The people was for Heidegger the body of "a kind of Being that
has grown under a common fate and taken distinctive shape within
a *single* State."[33] Finally, Heidegger saw the people as the vehicle for
a distinctive way of being, unconcealed from natural *physis.* This
communitarian *Dasein* was embodied in the state, since only to the
members of a state the territorial space was "disclosed" in a special
way. In the aforementioned seminar, Heidegger demonstrated the
need for the Germans who remained outside the state to be integrated in such a way that they would not lose their original being,
due to a community organization that was foreign to their truth, in
a culture and language that were different from their original disclosure. In this sense, blood and inheritable characteristics were
secondary elements in Heidegger's ontological nationalism.

---

[31] Heidegger, *Nature, History, State*, 41.
[32] Ibid., 74.
[33] Ibid., 72.

The question of "who are we?" pondered particularly in the seminar *Logic as the Question Concerning the Essence of Language*, in the first volume of the *Black Notebooks*, in *Nature, History, State*, and in *On Hegel's Philosophy of Right*, has been the most political expression of Polemos. To consider people, culture, and identity as products of polemological difference was an ontological matter of discussion that went even beyond the debate on science and the studies on race that were ongoing during those years. The people as a "we" was determined by a common truth and way of being, founded by conflict within the Being. From that originated a "we," a people and its spatiotemporal points of reference, the organized community or state.

POLEMOS AND POLITICS

At the end of 1934 Heidegger delivered a seminar that was even more political than *Nature, History, State.* It was the seminar on the philosophy of right in Hegel. By the hands of the idealist philosopher Heidegger, a true political philosophy based on Hegel's thought in Heraclitean key began to develop; a statist thought of Hegelian conception which he established in his seminars on Hölderlin that was "fueled" "by a new, productively repeating execution of Heraclitus's primary thoughts," as Peter Trawny, a commenter on the text, noted.[34]

Trawny also points out several times that the "dialogue" between Hegel and Heidegger could correspond to a certain similarity that the latter wanted to establish with the former. Hegel was the great philosopher of the state as a spiritual entity, a position that earned him the crown as the official thinker of the political philosophy conducted by the Prussian state of his period, something that Heidegger certainly sought to emulate.

The complete text of the seminar was lost, along with the one from the preceding semester. Yet, the notes written personally by Heidegger and his assistants have survived. The great subject of this class was the concept of politics, right at a time when the National Socialist revolution was rekindling the political theory related to the relationship between the people, the state, and the nation.

According to the Heideggerian interpretation, Polemos was the foundation of the political. Polemos revealed a communitarian "being" which had to be cared for by the state. "Care" (*sorge*) is a term that was already of fundamental importance in *Being and Time.* Care

---

[34] Heidegger, *On Hegel's Philosophy of Right*, 3.

expressed in the form of "polemological" politics was not related to the physical care or preservation of a people, but to the taking care of its "being," the "being of the people in the State." "[C]are is fundamentally an engagement in the question of *who* we are," stated Richard Polt, interpreter of the cryptic notes concerning the seminar left by Heidegger.[35] Care intended as a "political existential is derived from the 'struggle,' i.e. from πόλεμος [Polemos],"[36] and firstly expressed as stateliness, mastery, and rank of those who are the caregivers and wardens of the Being: the leaders and their state. Secondly, care manifested itself as the work conducted by a people.[37] Thirdly, it was expressed as the truth that was rooted in "nature—soil—blood—homeland—landscape—Gods—death."[38] Lastly, in Heidegger's view, care was defined as finiteness or the experience of death as a means of experiencing time and, therefore, the historical *Dasein* of a people, since time is only comprehensible to beings who have the awareness of limit.

According to Heideggerian polemology, the essence of the political was "the existence of the state as a historical being-in-the-world," as Michael Marder, another contemporary commentator of the seminar, explains. [39] Hence the state was a historical being, a differentiated way of being,[40] and a fissure in the Being—Polt describes it

---

[35] Polt, "Self-Assertion as Founding." In Heidegger, *On Hegel's Philosophy of Right*, 73.

[36] Trawny, "Heidegger, Hegel, and the Political." In Heidegger, *On Hegel's Philosophy of Right*, 16.

[37] The commentators of the seminar's notes see a correlation with the theories of Ernst Jünger in *The Worker*. (Ibid., 7–8).

[38] Heidegger, *On Hegel's Philosophy of Right*, 16.

[39] Marder, "The Question of Political Existence: Hegel, Heidegger, and Schmidt." In Heidegger, *On Hegel's Philosophy of Right*, 44.

[40] The foundation of politics was related to the self-affirmation of the being of the people, according to Heidegger, and from this alone arose the identity which generated difference and with it the categories of friend and enemy. This opposed Carl Schmitt's definition, who precisely started the other way around by asserting that "the concept of the political" depended on the friend-enemy relationship from which identity arose. Both thinkers reached these conclusions as a result of their polemological meditations. In this context, Schmitt sent Heidegger a copy of his book *The Concept of the Political* in 1933, with a dedication in which he remarked on their mutual interest in Polemos.

as "a wound that cannot heal"—caused by Polemos' conflict and con-frontation. [41] "*State* as beyng of the people. Certainly—but what does *beyng* mean? Beyng and fissure (conflict and πόλεμος [Polemos])."[42]

---

[41] This analogy made by Polt is reminiscent of the Celtic-Germanic myth of King Arthur's wound that cannot heal, the partition of the Being. (Polt, "Self-Assertion as Founding." In Heidegger, *On Hegel's Philosophy of Right*, 77).

[42] Heidegger, *On Hegel's Philosophy of Right*, 142.

THE HERACLITEAN WORLDVIEW

Heidegger's philosophy of those years is useful to understand his adhesion to German nationalism. The philosophical concepts described above laid the foundation for the elaboration of a particular political philosophy, which sought to position itself as the official worldview of the National Socialist state, something it ultimately failed to achieve due to the internal power struggles between the academia and the state. Heidegger recognized that the National Socialist revolution, being so extreme in its anti-liberal spirit, offered the chance to bring about the beginning of a new polemological culture, in the truest sense of the word. Heidegger "saw in the emergence of National Socialism and in its search for a form of life the possibility of another beginning," as Marcia Sá Cavalcante explains.[43]

However, the revolutionary radicalism of National Socialism was not the only thing that, in Heidegger's eyes, made it possible for it to bring to realization the plan for the "destruction of Western metaphysics." "The father of all things" was a phrase which was extensively used by National Socialist intellectuals and ideologues; therefore, there were certainly deep philosophical roots connecting Heidegger with National Socialism.

Heideggerian philosophy was situated in a historical-political process of the revitalization of heroic culture and agonal thought. Of course, not many intellectuals associated with the National Socialist centers of thought reached the ontological conception quoted previously, but it is undeniable that the ideological departments of

---

[43] Schuback, "Philosophy without Right? Some Notes on Heidegger's Notes for the 1934/35 'Hegel Seminar.'" In Heidegger, *On Hegel's Philosophy of Right*, 88.

National Socialism sought, like Heidegger, to unravel what they called "the Heraclitean worldview." So did several other nationalist movements in Europe, during the great crisis of the interwar period. Fried did not ignore this fact. In his opinion, Heidegger's Polemos led directly to the political situation of the great crisis of the twentieth century, the rise of the so-called fascisms and their opposition to the liberal political project.

> Heidegger's polemos addresses to us a question about the meaning of fascism, or, more precisely, about the problem *announced by* fascism, which I take to be the question of the limits of belonging and universalism in the modern age. . . . Beyond Heidegger's own thinking, what announces itself in fascism is the enduring problem of identity and difference, of belonging and exclusion, of universalism and particularity. . . . Heidegger understands the proper relation of peoples to be one of Polemos.[44]

Fried's quote refers to the spirit of the time of that moment, a historical phase of the decline of liberalism; of crisis and wars, but also of the resurgence of a new spirituality that sought to ponder existentially. This is perhaps the reason why intellectuals such as Heidegger, Carl Schmitt, Ernst Jünger, and Alfred Bäumler, but also politicians and poets, searched for answers in Heraclitus and, especially, in Polemos to the great problems that originated from the crisis of the early twentieth century. The search for a metaphysical meaning behind struggle led several of Europe's most outstanding intellectuals to examine classical cultures for answers to a way of being human different from that presented by the myths of liberalism, a way of being that did not hide or try to reject the agonal nature of man, but instead acknowledged that the polemological character of the human soul should be tempered, accepted and understood completely, just as the ancient Greeks did in their myths about both the good and the evil Eris. If this was not done, conflict would be

---

[44] Fried, *Heidegger's Polemos*, 4, 7, 18.

suppressed, leading to a maddening discordance between the nature of man and an artificial society. This was the critique that the nationalist intellectuals directed at the liberal system, and it was probably the key to the union of the Heideggerian polemological project with the National Socialist revolution.

However, this should not cause any confusion about the character of Heidegger's philosophy. It was not properly National Socialist—although Heidegger was a member of the party and, at a certain moment, even of the state—because it was not particularly focused on biological or evolutionary matters. Yet polemology was aligned with National Socialism, and furthermore Heidegger tried to influence the worldview of National Socialism so that the importance of biological factors, including the people as an entity—the main aspect of National Socialist politics—would be replaced, instead placing on top his "being of the people," and the relation, through Polemos, of this "being" with the "Being" in its totality.

THE RETURN OF THE ANCIENT GOD

It would be fair to claim that Heidegger was the one who crowned a process of cultural revolution, led by the various anti-liberal forces of the early twentieth century. He accomplished this by reaching the highest peaks of ontological thought, in order to bring a radical cultural change, which is what the anti-system political forces of the time demanded. He also managed to achieve this because he was the sharpest thinker of one of the most radical anti-liberal concepts of the time, the so-called "life as a struggle" proclaimed by many revolutionary nationalisms as the antithesis of universalist mercantilism.

The revolutionary nationalist theories of the interwar period were the first in the twentieth century to design a political roadmap for a new type of society, in which the supremacy of mercantilism and cosmopolitanism would be superseded by cultures that were closer to nature, by communitarian solidarity, and by heroic sentiment. This assertion was at first rather undetermined or, in other words, significantly instinctive and visceral. It lacked the complexity which Heidegger's polemological ontology subsequently achieved. However, this Heideggerian conceptualization would not have been possible without the entrance of the political revolutionaries and the veterans of the Great War, who had experienced the most terrible side of Polemos by fighting in the streets and in the trenches of Europe, and who had also brought this hierarchical, heroic, meritocratic and popular experience—the "trenchocracy" mentioned by Mussolini[45]—into the new political movements that aimed to put an end to European liberalism. It is from there that Polemos emerged,

---

[45] Mussolini, "Trenchocracy."

37

from the experience of blood and mud, thus displaying initially its most terrible side. Following that, with the constitution of revolutionary political movements and by means of philosophical contemplation, it would finally consolidate itself completely.

According to Zeev Sternhell, a scholar of fascism, in the late nineteenth century the French revolutionary movements started a process of revisionism that ultimately induced several of their members to cut ties with Marxism. Tired of waiting for the mechanical and materialistic dialectical synthesis that the prophecies of Marxism predicted would lead almost automatically to revolution, the Frenchman Georges Sorel decided to take action by means of human will. Thus, the Sorelian Marxist heresy was conceived, which sought to overcome the boundary between proletarians and the rest of society, inviting all those forces, regardless of their class, to engage in a process of social change that had the heroic myth as its philosophical foundation.

Sorel was the first to establish heroic struggle as a revolutionary force and a political tool. Sternhell stated that heroic violence was, in Sorel's view, a way of counteracting bourgeois violence, violence that the French revolutionary believed had made all beauty and heroism disappear, that had turned European societies into degenerate cultures lacking in vitality. Heroic violence, on the contrary, helped to "maintain the light in the ancient world."[46] Sorel believed that the true revolution against the liberal bourgeois order would be effective only if the West restored its own tradition, including heroic socialism, fellowship in arms, and the culture of life as a struggle.

> The whole of classical history is dominated by the idea of war conceived heroically; in their origin, the institutions of the Greek republics had as their basis the organization of armies of citizens; Greek art reached its apex in the citadels; philosophers conceived of no other possible form of education than that which fostered in youth the heroic tradition. . . . [S]ocial

---

[46] Quoted in Sternhell, *The Birth of Fascist Ideology*, 66.

utopias were created with a view to maintaining a nucleus of homeric warriors in the cities, etc.[47]

Edouard Berth, French successor to Sorel, recognized the need for the creation of a new philosophy of life and a new hierarchy of values capable of overcoming the abstract formulas that characterized the political ideologies of modernity. Berth deemed Nietzsche and Proudhon to be the prophets of the new heroic morality of unionism, the true and only viable socialism, where conflict was "the most profound, most sublime phenomenon of our moral life."[48]

At the same time, the cult of boldness, dynamism, and the beauty of struggle found an aesthetic and political outlet in Italy, with the ideas of the poet and ideologist Filippo Tommaso Marinetti and his groundbreaking Futurist movement. This ode to heroism, which preceded the Great War, resonated with groups such as the Italian Sorelians, nationalist revolutionaries, and disillusioned socialists such as Mussolini.

Futurism captivated an entire generation of political adventurers, eager to take new revolutionary paths. It described struggle as hygiene, as an educative force, and an agent of transformation and change, words that were most valued by nonconformist revolutionaries. Progress was defined as the consequence of struggle and not as a cold economic game. Hierarchy was on the basis of achievement, competence, will, and heroism, rather than class privilege, wealth, or influence. Futurism charmed with its nationalistic and Nietzschean socialism, which expressed itself poetically with an avant-garde aesthetic, a quality that placed it above the cold and monotonous rhetoric of professional politicians.

Except in struggle, there is no more beauty. No work without an aggressive character can be a masterpiece. Poetry must be conceived as a violent attack on unknown forces, to reduce and prostrate them before man. . . . We will glorify war—the world's only hygiene—militarism, patriotism, the destructive

---

[47] Sorel, *Reflections on Violence*, 160.
[48] Quoted in Sternhell, *The Birth of Fascist Ideology*, 117.

gesture of freedom-bringers, beautiful ideas worth dying for.[49]

Just as the French and Italians saw in the revolutionary political struggles an underlying principle that transcended social violence, glimpsing the ontological concept of life as a struggle, the Germans also understood that the destructive aspect of conflict had a profoundly existential side.

The experience of the Great War affected Germanic thinkers and poets, whose studies revolved around the concept of the transforming force which lies hidden within conflicts. However, among many chronicles and memoirs of war, only a few of them managed to go beyond the limited themes of war and destruction. It is true that several authors managed to portray in great detail the pain and suffering, and even describe introspectively what an experience of confrontation such as that of trench warfare meant, but few were those who delved deeper into this experience.

By the end of the nineteenth century, Friedrich von Bernhardi, a German strategist and general, had already begun to outline an ontology of conflict in which he quoted the Heraclitean fragment. At the same time, Carl Schmitt explored in depth and with great intuition the existential meaning of conflict. In order to understand his political science, which is based on the relationship between friend and enemy, Schmitt suggests that "the word conflict is to be understood ... in terms of its original essence,"[50] referring specifically to the 53rd fragment of Heraclitus. Likewise, the writer and veteran Ernst Jünger stated that struggle was an inner experience much more spiritual than the sole participation in an armed conflict. In his work from 1922, *War as an Inner Experience*, Jünger followed the example of thinkers such as Nietzsche, Schmitt, or Heidegger, understanding life as a struggle and heroic ethics as an alternative to the individualistic bourgeois culture, detached from natural laws:

---

[49] Marinetti, "Manifesto of Futurism."
[50] Schmitt, *The Concept of the Political*, 15.

War, the father of all things, is also our father. It has hammered, chiseled, and tempered us into what we are.... He raised us to fight, so we will be warriors as long as we live.... War ... is a law of nature, therefore we can never escape its spell. We must not deny it, or it will devour us.[51]

To Jünger, struggle was "our true blood," concealed under the "magical and shiny embellishments" that mankind intended to decorate human existence with. So, if life was a constant struggle, then the ideology of pacifism—the ethics of the refusal to fight—was to Jünger something which went against nature, since essential conflict is present in every moment of life.

---

[51] Jünger, *Der Kampf als inneres Erlebnis*, 3–4, 36. Translated by Giammarco Simonelli.

LIFE AS A STRUGGLE

It is undeniable that Polemos, the father of all things, returned to reign briefly in national populist Europe. Ernesto Giménez Caballero, a Spanish Falangist intellectual who witnessed this process, was one of the first to understand this fundamental relationship. According to Caballero, "Fascism" embodied the most essential elements of the Stoic tradition, passed on from Seneca, Petrarch, Leon Battista Alberti, Machiavelli, Montaigne, and Nietzsche up to Mussolini:

> A genuine characteristic—perhaps the purest—of Fascism is that of considering life as a struggle. I maintain that Fascism has its roots in Stoicism and, specifically, in Seneca. "Fascism conceptualizes life as a struggle," declared Mussolini. "War is the life of man on earth," stated Seneca. "To us fascists, life is a constant and endless struggle which we embrace with great bravery." Senecan thought in its purest essence. "The very first thing I would advise is to remember once and many times that the entire life of mortals is nothing but a perpetual war," a great interpreter of Seneca wrote during the Renaissance.[52]

Mussolini during the Great War adopted a realistic outlook on life which assimilated the dynamism of combat as a key element of human existence. Life as a struggle (*Vita come Lotta*), heroic will, warrior ethics, and action as a spiritual dimension were the key concepts of the Fascist worldview. War, in Mussolini's view, forced an

---

[52] Caballero, "Séneca o los fundamentos estoicos," Translated by Giammarco Simonelli.

entire generation to understand the true nature of the world. It was not about being good soldiers and learning the trade of the combatant. Rather, Mussolini believed that the Great War had been a transforming spiritual experience. So, it was in war that the conflictive aspect of the world became painfully clear to those minds that were oblivious to the dynamics of nature.

To Mussolini, life was nothing but struggle and, paraphrasing Heraclitus, he declared that "struggle is at the bottom of all things, because life is full of contrasts."[53] From the point of view of Mussolini, to stop struggling was, also, to stop living: life and struggle were synonyms. "To give up struggle is to give up life."[54] Fascist doctrine defined struggle as motion, progress, and overcoming, the things that drive history forward and animate the human soul. In contrast, the Duce considered stillness and conservatism to be signs of low vitality and death. "We fascists reject any static concept of material or moral happiness. Our happiness is in the struggle."[55]

Continuing the warrior mysticism of Fascism, National Socialism created its own version of a polemological culture. The National Socialist worldview was based on the "laws of life" (*Lebensgesetz*), of which the most important was the law of struggle (*Kampfgesetz*). In the same way as Heraclitus did, this belief was considered by them as the universal and essential foundation of the totality of the beings on earth.

Along the same lines, Alfred Bäumler—who would eventually be crowned as the philosopher of National Socialism—devoted much of his research to Heraclitus and the concept of Polemos, establishing a philosophical genealogy between National Socialism and the thinker of Ephesus, and placing as a bridge between these the work of Nietzsche, who was perhaps the most celebrated thinker in the Germany of Hitler. Originating from the philosophical academia, the concept of "struggle as the father of all things" reached the cultural institutions and, from there, it was then discussed in articles, magazines, and books that specialized in a wide variety of fields.

---

[53] Mussolini, "Speech in Trieste."
[54] Mussolini, "Prime basi dello Stato corporativo." Translated by Giammarco Simonelli.
[55] Mussolini, *Opera Omnia*, vol. 26, 25–26. Translated by Giammarco Simonelli.

THE DESTRUCTION OF THE WEST

The military defeat of the Axis during World War II not only brought the European political project of nationalism to an end but also halted the process of reappraisal of pre-Socratic thought and the attempts of instituting it as a new cultural foundation for the West. So, the competition for material and cultural control went on between liberalism and Marxism, both having their respective worldview and conception of man.

As the Cold War proceeded, several leftist European intellectuals, who were outside the area of influence of the USSR, understood that the hegemony of liberalism was consolidating itself more and more, while Marxism was showing signs of decline that foretold its imminent fall. Because of this, they undertook the task of formulating a concise critique of the methods adopted by Marxism, as well as of the system of Western capitalist societies. In order to achieve their task, this group of intellectuals reclaimed the philosophical legacy of the young Marx[56]—not the older and more political Marx who created communism, a theory that they severely criticized—and combined it with schools of thought such as the Critical Theory of the Frankfurt School, the Vienna Psychoanalytic Society, and the school of anthropology associated with Franz Boas and Claude Lévi-Strauss. It was from the synthesis of these theories that existentialism, structuralism, post-structuralism, post-modernism, and deconstructionism—all belonging to the so-called French school—emerged, along with other schools of thought. This great movement

---

[56] Diego Fusaro argued that the young Marx represented a philosophical branch of the idealist current.

has commonly been referred to—despite the complaints of its exponents—simply as "post-modernism" and, more recently, "progressivism."

In the long list of their intellectual predecessors, some exponents of the French School, such as Sartre or Derrida, had found in Heidegger and Nietzsche the ideas that were needed for their desired deconstruction of the foundations of the West. Nietzschean perspectivism and the destruction of dualistic metaphysics served as important philosophical tools, with which it was possible to bring the critique of liberal societies to the extreme. However, the postmodernist plan suffered from the same flaws as the other schools of thought related to it. It included a hidden individualism and materialism—derived from the critique to Soviet collectivism—as well as a completely modern way of understanding human freedom that clashed with Heideggerian, Nietzschean, and, ultimately, Heraclitean principles. This ultimately caused the deconstructionist project to dissolve in the waters of the hegemonic liberal system. The most recent epigones of the postmodernist movement, due to a lack of thinkers of intellectual importance and academic discipline, have devoted themselves to a meaningless political deconstructionism, becoming easy targets for the elites of neoliberal globalism.

With the incursions of Lacan and Derrida in the domain of polemology, which they used as a tool to philosophically destroy "capitalist" culture, the post-structuralist and deconstructionist intellectuals embarked on a path that they failed to follow through with, losing themselves in the intricate question of the synthesis between ontological radicality and the sanitized libertarian conceptions of modern culture. Soon, liberal freedom, libertarianism, and often libertinism pervaded the deconstructionist project. By the 1970s the thin line between postmodernist individualism and mercantile individualism was already blurred. By the beginning of the twenty-first century, financial globalism, cosmopolitanism, and progressivism supported cultural projects which had an obvious common ground. Perhaps the archetype of this impossible union was Michael Foucault.[57]

---

[57] See Bousquet, *"Putain" de Saint Foucault.*

The search for answers in the polemological philosophies of Nietzsche and Heidegger undertaken by the French school, however, was not illogical. Both of the projects of overcoming of the West—Marxism and liberalism—considered the world to be a malleable mass, subjected to the human will. However, while postmodernism questioned the role of the becoming, raising doubts about the truth of cultural narratives and, therefore, encouraging a permanent nihilistic critique of all tradition and certainties, Heidegger and Nietzsche did not consider the becoming as an invitation to destroy and discredit culture simply because it lacked a transcendental truth. The nature of the becoming, instead, encouraged to build—to unconceal—with a heroic and conscious will narratives that would serve as cultural dams that restrained the dissolving force of the undifferentiated waters. "[T]here is in us a power to order, simplify, falsify, artificially distinguish. . . . The form counts as something enduring and therefore more valuable; but the form has merely been invented by us."[58]

The struggle of the Nietzschean warrior was not based on abstraction, skepticism, pessimism, and relativism—as some ideologues of postmodernist subjectivism have tried to suggest—but on natural laws that defined his actions and established firm boundaries that allowed for the development of objective truths, scientific ideas, and cultural traditions. By giving Being to becoming, and appearance to perceptual undifferentiation, Nietzsche, for instance, did not mean to fall into a dissolving and destructive attitude that would leave reality in a liquid state, free from the ups and downs of the becoming, but quite the opposite. It was, in fact, an attitude that called for fixing chaos, coagulating the becoming, and constantly creating in order to build solid foundations for progress, culture, and tradition. "To impose upon becoming the character of being—that is the supreme will to power. . . . 'Beings' as appearance; reversal of values."[59]

But the hero, who innately gave order to chaos, could not inhibit this compulsion, so once the order was established, he tore it down

---

[58] Nietzsche, *The Will to Power*, 280, 282.
[59] Ibid., 330.

so he could rearrange it once again. As this compulsion impelled to create limits, it also urged not to be satisfied with what had just been created, but to surpass it again by creating something new, and to engage in new struggles to facilitate human life and preservation. This ability to dissolve and establish perpetually enabled man to adapt to nature, and to carry on the struggle for existence which is always ongoing. Nietzsche called this process "Creative Destruction," an essential part of his philosophical concept of the "Will to Power." In order to put an end to the static Being of the West and its transcendentalism, Nietzsche's plan was to return to the Being in motion of Greek culture. The Beings, in Nietzsche's conception, were constantly changing, a perpetual cycle of conquests and defeats: nature was never static. "Dasein's authentic existence as polemos is always both a deconstruction and a reconstruction," observed Fried.[60] Heidegger summarizes this process as establishing an order to chaos with logical knowledge, and then converting it into artistic thought. These processes were described by Nietzsche in two chapters of his work *The Will to Power*, titled "The Will to Power as Knowledge" and "The Will to Power as Art," both themes that were discussed in homonymous seminars given by Heidegger during the years of World War II.

So polemological destruction is creative, while postmodern deconstruction is nihilistic, not creative, and always undifferentiated. In place of the process through which the act of the creative will produces a fundamental truth—an unconcealed world—and destroys what is old and outdated in order to create new forms, postmodernism seemed to engage in a process of dissolution in which deconstruction takes place without the plan for a renewal that would make something new emerge from the ruins of the culture it seeks to destroy with such determination. Hence come the ravings of postmodernism and its fall into the hands of neoliberalism.

The tendency to dissolve and homogenize all sorts of narratives has caused today's culture, which is dominated by postmodern deconstruction and the globalist financial economy, to remain permanently undifferentiated, ill-defined, and in a liquid, amorphous

---

[60] Fried, *Heidegger's Polemos*, 17.

state. It is the triumph of the not-being, of the non-territory. In present-day culture, difference and identity are less and less appreciated, being replaced instead by an increasing appraisal of concepts such as "symmetry," "egalitarianism," or "transparency."

This cultural and spiritual process has been recognized by several intellectuals. Zygmunt Bauman has labeled it "liquid modernity."[61] Fredric Jameson links it to the disappearance of the concrete, to the "death of the subject."[62] The philosopher Byung-Chul Han has defined this era as the "age of transparency."[63]

---

[61] Bauman, *Liquid Modernity*.
[62] Jameson, *Postmodernism*.
[63] See Han, *The Transparency Society*.

THE VIOLENCE OF TRANSPARENCY

Liquid modernity has produced an overwhelming symmetry, creating the greatest identity crisis ever recorded. Postmodern identity has been classified as an eternal adolescence. The postmodern "I" is a *collage* of identities that prevents the preservation of definite normative models. One of the most characteristic negative effects of this situation is the categorization of the individuals according to social roles or other traditional identity elements, which is clearly an obstacle to the creation of cohesive communities. According to Alain de Benoist, the current era of homogenization is based on arbitrariness and abstract subjectivism.

Even though Nietzsche and Heidegger, among others, explored the complexity of consciousness and its connection to realms which are "external" to it—such as cultural contexts and the territory—as well as the elements hidden from consciousness and overlooked by modernist rationalism—such as the unconscious or the experience—their research was aimed at gaining an understanding of the Self and the layers that formed it. In the end, these explorations enriched and strengthened the experience of existence.

On the contrary, Postmodernism disrupted and disintegrated the experience of identity, in particular through psychoanalysis, creating a new way of understanding the individual. The "Postmodern Subject" is a new way of interacting with and thinking about oneself, a criterion based on doubt toward any statement of truth. Hence, the tendency of postmodernist intellectuals and artists to dissolve the concept of location, to avoid coordinate systems, and to declare that certainty is an anti-value. Derrida, for example, urged to give up "logocentrism" in order to shift the Self to the "margins"; that is to say, to the zones outside of the center of gravity that gives cohesion

51

to the identity. According to Bauman, who coined the term "liquid modernity," the modern Subject has ceased to be represented at the center of discourse in order to set it free from its stability and thus to not "keep its identity intact, but forever 'becoming,' avoiding completion, staying undefined."[64] The Age of Transparency, as Han termed it, is an era in which the lack of difference and identity transforms everything into something undefined and shapeless, where things "prove transparent when they shed all negativity, when they are smoothed out and leveled, when they do not resist being integrated into smooth streams of capital, communication, and information."[65]

And despite the individualistic freedom invoked by postmodernism, the lack of negativity and conflict, and the pacifist and libertarian morality, the present age also hides a type of violence, the violence of transparency, which according to Han is "a systemic compulsion gripping all social processes and subjecting them to a deep-reaching change,"[66] a compulsion that "flattens out the human being itself, making it a functional element within a system."[67] As Han explains, the lack of conflict and the tendency to deconstruct the "I" have led to the "dictatorship of symmetry." Alain de Benoist calls it "dictatorship of the same" while Diego Fusaro refers to it as the "open society." Transparency, absence of limits, and complete openness are cultural ideas that have modified societies and, consequently, human relations. "Only machines are transparent," stated Han.[68] The "postmodern condition" is the one in which identities merge, where "the other" becomes an analogy of "the same," and where difference ceases to be meaningful. The result, far from being the formation of a homogeneous and peaceful humanity, is the fragmentation into millions of subjective identities that cause increased tensions in societies, preventing the communal cohesion which is needed to work toward a common future. This, in addition

---

[64] Bauman, *Liquid Modernity*.
[65] Han, *The Transparency Society*, 1.
[66] Ibid., 2.
[67] Ibid., 3.
[68] Ibid.

to problems related to the individual, has led to a weakening of national sovereignty, which has clearly benefited a globalized mercantile order characterized by a false social equality, where money "makes it possible to equate anything with anything else,"[69] as Han points out.

---

[69] Ibid., 2.

THE HEROIC HEART

Postmodernism, as its disciples claim, has marked the decline of modernity and its myths, in particular authoritarianism and totalitarianism. With these precepts, the postmodern solution to modernity carried the promise of long-lasting world peace. In order to carry out this cultural project, the deconstruction of polemological *Dasein* was certainly necessary. To achieve this deconstruction, it was preferable to base it on the transformation of the cultural normative archetypes related to the agonal culture, to the hero. The ancient Homeric hero, the warrior and savior of the people, the bearer of the *arete* who represented the ultimate example of virtue, has fallen from grace. The researcher Tod Lindberg indicates that there is a clear political objective behind this deconstruction, an educational and communicational plan to convert the hero from the agonal perspective to a liberal one. The hero, in his role of conqueror and destroyer (*slayer hero*), was turned into a savior (*saving hero*) in mercantilist societies. This is an important change. The modern hero—and this is not about actual heroes but about the formative ideal—is egalitarian and does not seek to achieve greatness (*arete*). According to Lindberg, this plan has been designed to reinforce liberal culture, which needs to eliminate any reference to polemological or agonal figures. This is a rejection of what, recalling Nietzsche or Heidegger, he describes as "a vision of a higher type of human life than one organized around pleasure and gain,"[70] a vision in which the Nietzschean overman or the Jüngerian *landsknecht* presented themselves as archetypes of a lost way of life, an ideal in which also "Heidegger sought philosophical refuge in a rejection of

---

[70] Lindberg, *The Heroic Heart*, Chapter 8.

the Cartesian individualism of Western metaphysics and a radical confrontation with Being."[71]

The deconstruction of the hero has been justified with the promise of a freer and more peaceful world, where wars and conquests are left behind in the interest of commercial peace. Despite all this, war and violence have not diminished but, as Dominique Venner said, "the age of commerce has imposed itself, certainly, but with an increase in the number of wars." It is an age without heroes, where Polemos no longer reigns, and where "the military establishment has strengthened . . . more than ever."[72] Alain de Benoist agreed on the paradoxical nature of this situation: postmodern and neoliberal societies, which strive to hide the natural reality of conflict, now rely more than in any other historical period on the army as a solution to conflicts derived from global economism. Under the postmodern liberal order, war has simply evolved to become anti-polemological and anti-heroic, laying out its mercantile and moralistic foundations based on the dualism of good and evil, where the enemy is the absolute evil that must be eradicated, and not an essential element that completes an existential friend-enemy relationship. Thus, the French intellectual drew conclusions that are similar to those of Heidegger, determining that polemological culture and the archetype of the hero are the nemesis of the myths of liberal culture. "The action of the warrior is by nature antiliberal and anti-mercantile. . . . The economical *optimum* is equilibrium; the polemological optimum, is disequilibrium."[73] According to de Benoist, liberal countries "are not able to conceive war nor reason 'normally' in a polemological way."

Another intellectual who questioned the effects that the lack of agonistic expression can have on Western democratic societies is Jennifer Gagnon, a political scientist who argued that the sterilization of the Greek *Agon* is a cultural principle. In her view, Greek agonal theory "places [itself] . . . in opposition to communitarian and liberal theories."[74] Contemporary political debate and the values it

---

[71] Ibid.

[72] Venner, "L'homme de guerre et la cité." Translated by Giammarco Simonelli.

[73] Benoist, "Ni fraîche ni joyeuse." Translated by Giammarco Simonelli.

[74] Gagnon, "Agonistic Politics," 11.

transmits to society ignore the fundamental aspect of life as a struggle and its interpretation as the natural order of existence and not as a mere formula for personal gain. The ancient Greek citizens who debated in courts, councils, and assemblies took as much pleasure in the act of confrontation as an Olympic athlete who competed for victory. A true representative of the Agon found more fulfillment in the struggle than in the "stable" tranquility of victory.

The great open society of the globalist West has certainly kept Polemos, the Being as conflict, hidden away from culture and existential experience. However, the intellectual Pierre Krebs argues that the polemological spirit has never ceased to unfold. This is the so-called "fighting for the essence," also sustained by a long list of thinkers and philosophers who have preserved the myth up to the present days. According to Krebs, the pre-dualistic, pre-Socratic thought, typical of the Greek culture from which the Heraclitean Polemos emerged, has been preserved by "heretics" such as "Pelagius, Storm, Hebbel, Rilke, Eriugena, Giordano Bruno, Hölderlin, Meister Eckhart, Nicholas of Cusa, Jacob Böhme, Goethe, Beethoven, Teilhard de Chardin, Saint-Exupéry, and Heidegger,"[75] who have kept alive the profound meaning of nature, the experience of Being which, as Krebs rightly claims, comes from "archaisms . . . that are anterior to the models of thought of Greek philosophy."[76]

The polemological Being is, as Krebs describes it, a way of interpreting the world:

> [T]he differentialist intelligence of the world . . . it accords with the natural laws of life, proceeds from a multi-dimensional perception essentially open to the Universal. . . . [It] perceives the world in the unity of its opposites, in this mystery of the harmony that the Greeks perceived in the movement of balance and in the oscillation of differences that attract and complete one another—and that Heraclitus defined thus: "Opposition brings concord. Out of discord comes

---

[75] Krebs, *Fighting for the Essence.*
[76] Ibid.

the fairest harmony. . . . All things come to pass through the compulsion of strife."[77]

The struggle for the essence is the return to the pre-Socratic and "pre-Western" tradition, a project for society which is much more radical than the postmodernist raving. It is a return to human nature, and an ontology that allows to gather all the positive elements of the spirit of instinctual struggle, while establishing rules to keep its destructive aspect under control. This is not nostalgia of a better past, but progress through aspects of human nature that have been repressed, although necessary for a becoming that is truthful to the Self of man.

> The values of combat have been considered as positive values, appropriate to build character, to induce bravery, to encourage self-sacrifice. . . . This worldview is in conformity with reality, just as we are able to understand it. Modern ethology and biology have shown, for example, the general and innate character of the impulse of aggression in living beings (and particularly in human species), and, moreover, the importance of the behaviors involved in hunting and war in the phylogenetic formation of humanity, as basic criteria of natural selection and orientation of evolution. . . . The polemological worldview is nothing more than the intuitive comprehension of the dialectic character of existence, of this relentless conflict of oppositions. Heraclitus was among the first authors to bring this to light: *polemos pater panton* (conflict is the father of all things).[78]

---

[77] Ibid.
[78] Benoist, "Ni fraîche ni joyeuse." Translated by Giammarco Simonelli.

THE AGONAL CULTURE

The polemological philosophical principle, perhaps the only one capable of opposing the globalist liberalism of the left and the right on a spiritual level, did not emerge as an abstract idea, but it rather has its roots in nature and in the most primordial way of being human. It is a cultural and spiritual tradition with biological roots, product of the gradual adaptation of the instincts that developed during the course of the evolutionary process. Heidegger was its most brilliant exponent during the twentieth century; however, it is still fair to say that the German thinker never connected his ontology to biological elements.

"The polemological worldview is nothing more than the intuitive comprehension of the dialectic character of existence," as Alain de Benoist explained; a worldview "in conformity with reality," validated by biology and ethology. So the polemological worldview would be the impulse of the instinct to fight for existence, which was consequently adopted culturally in the societies of hunters and warriors "as basic criteria of natural selection and orientation of evolution." Polemological ontology and polemological biological instincts are linked by a close bond.

If one wants to understand thoroughly the Heraclitean ontology of Heidegger or the efforts of thinkers such as Nietzsche, Bäumler, Schmitt, Jünger, de Benoist, and numerous others, it is important to understand the historical evolution of the cultural meaning of Polemos. Ever since the appearance of the primitive instinct to fight for existence, continuing with the birth of the culture of warriors and then of the agonal tradition of the classical era, Polemos has undergone a process of assimilation through various stages. At times he has been understood as a god who is both father and ruler, at other

59

times only as the grim face of war, death, and disgrace. Up until the "return to the original conception" pursued by Heidegger, Polemos has been a mystery throughout the whole human history.

Nietzsche believed that modern man has concealed the true aspect of his own foundation and natural essence. Indeed, an unbiased glance at the laws of nature reveals a reality that has been neglected in the cultural foundations of modern society. The philosopher of the will to power considered the agonal and conflictive nature of man as the great source of vital energy that allowed for the development, progress, and preservation of the cultures of antiquity:

> When one speaks of *humanity*, underlying this idea is the belief that it is humanity which *separates* and distinguishes human beings from nature. But, there is, in reality, no such distinction: the "natural" qualities and those properly called "human" grow inseparably. The human, in his highest and noblest capacities, is wholly nature and bears within himself its uncanny dual character. Those abilities that are thought to be terrifying and inhuman are perhaps even the fruitful soil from which alone humanity can grow in emotions, deeds, and works.[79]

This terrible nature described by Nietzsche is the product of hundreds of thousands of years of evolution geared to the struggle for existence, which ultimately became part of the physical and psychological biology of mankind. In nature, perpetual change and the threats of the environment work against preservation at all times. Therefore, beings, groups of organisms, and species that do not fight will either adapt or be eliminated from the natural evolution. Biological and genetic adaptations are meant to generate mechanisms of defense against these assaults of the environment. The natural world is a place where the one who does not fight disappears individually, but also subtracts himself from the task of preservation, putting at risk the survival of his whole biological group. The eternal struggle for life in nature is a synonym for adaptation, specialization,

---

[79] Nietzsche, *Homer's Contest*, 1.

and victory. To humans, it also means cultural improvement and social wellbeing.

Jacques De Mahieu gave an account of the thousands of threats to the lifespan of man that can come from either the environment or the physical and psychological inside of man, and which in any case lead to decay. In De Mahieu's opinion, the miracle of a lasting lifespan could only be achieved through the ability to fight on every level. Life, therefore, was inextricably tied to the ability to struggle in order to preserve harmony and unity, considering that existence was generally precarious. The French anthropologist held that life deceives with its solidity, since the human psyche conceives only life or death, and in a critical situation preservation is the most immediate thing. However, organic unity requires a great effort, as intense at the cellular level as at the mental level, in such a way that, as de Mahieu explained, "we endure in and through a permanent struggle in defense of our functional order, and this struggle is the factor of the realization of our potential being; that is, the factor of our existence."[80]

---

[80] De Mahieu, *La naturaleza del hombre*. Translated by Giammarco Simonelli.

A DANGEROUS IDEA

It was not until Darwin's revolutionary ideas that the concept of life as a struggle found widespread diffusion in all sorts of cultural, scientific, and social circles. The "Theory of Evolution" influenced deeply the western society of the nineteenth century. Daniel Dennet, a philosopher of science at Harvard University, gave an account of the far-reaching impact of the English naturalist's theory. This new revolutionary idea was not the concept of evolution—which was already part of the culture in its metaphysical version, as a path to perfection and redemption—nor the idea that man descended from primitive living beings, a concept that existed already since the time of the ancient Greeks. The Darwinian idea that Western society found most difficult to accept was that nature is not governed by a universal mind or by some transcendental conscience, but that, independently of the idea of God's existence, nature was created with its own autonomous system for the development of beings and species. This mechanism was called by Darwin "natural selection by means of struggle for existence." Darwin's most dangerous idea was to indicate that struggle was the means by which nature created its most perfect and successful entities, a hierarchy that has man at the top of it. "Thus, from the war of nature, from famine and death, the most exalted object which we are capable of conceiving, namely, the production of the higher animals, directly follows."[81]

A mechanism that was autonomous, natural, based on struggle, and which could explain the formation and development of the variety of forms and species in the world was something truly revolutionary. Since Plato's times, questions to these concerns had been

---

[81] Darwin, *The Origin of Species*, Chapter XV.

answered with metaphysical arguments. Whether it was the Platonic ideas, the monads of Leibniz or the cosmic pyramid, all the ideas that were used to explain the emergence of shapes and species were based on the idea that forces beyond nature existed, forces which somehow mysteriously prompted the creation of life and its diversity.

Daniel Tompsett, a researcher of the Darwinian revolution, believes that the concept of evolution through the struggle for existence is, in a sense, the anthropological version of the philosophical principle of the Heraclitean Polemos. "The great and complex battle for life," "the war of nature," "the struggle for life," or "the preservation of the fittest"—not the strongest—these were all ideas that tied in nicely with the Heraclitean concept that "all things come into being and later perish through conflict." Tompsett emphasizes the fact that Heraclitus was a pre-Socratic thinker; that is, a thinker who pondered on the science of nature and not an abstract philosopher. Abstraction which would subsequently characterize philosophy. Therefore Polemos, in its ontological aspect, was not separated from its anthropological, biological, or sociological counterparts. For this reason, Darwin's idea of evolution has somehow taken the inverse path to that of the Heraclitean thought and from biology has reached all areas of social and cultural life. This is why the Darwinian theory was suppressed and deemed dangerous during the Victorian era in which it originated.

It was clear to Darwin's contemporary scientists that the idea of struggle and selection in nature was a revolutionary concept, and even more so if it were allowed to escaped from biology and out into the realm of philosophical and political ideas. Nevertheless, the attempt of the scientific world to contain Darwin's ideas did not work and soon the ancestral idea of struggle as the father of all things spread to the most disparate fields. Philosophy, ethics, politics, and religion had to confront the Darwinian idea that life is nothing but a great struggle for existence and that from this principle the greatest creations of nature are possible. Life as a struggle returned as a powerful philosophical concept which would be further elaborated in the most varied ways, from economic liberalism and its social Darwinism to the theorists of warcraft, socialist class struggle, nationalistic heroism, Nietzschean vitalistic heroism, and Heideggerian ontology.

ANATOMY OF STRUGGLE

The innate tendency of the human species to fight has been documented throughout history by anthropologists, archaeologists, and historians. Like any other species, humans have had to fight for food and living space, having to face environmental challenges and compete for resources. Within the community, they have had to fight for status and access to reproduction. Because of this, since very early on the creativity of the human mind developed instruments to facilitate preservation through struggle. The creation of weapons for offense and defense, discovered among archaeological findings linked to primitive hominids, shows the creative and technological effort directed toward combat during the distant times of the earliest stages of mankind.

Azar Gat, a military historian at several universities around the world, despite adhering to a position that tries to give to struggle a cultural rather than an instinctive character, has reported the constant discovery of elaborate weapons for fighting, as well as wounds produced by conflicts between humans, found on remains from all cultural stages of human history. The most ancient examples are the fifty-thousand-year-old remains of an individual with a premeditated knife wound in the chest, as well as twenty-nine remains dating back to the Paleolithic period showing fatal wounds inflicted during fights with combat weapons. In fact, Gat found violent wounds to be quite common throughout the European and Middle Eastern Paleolithic, with a frequency of forty percent in the totality of all human remains found. Violence and evidence of combat continue in the Mesolithic, where cave paintings depict clashes between increasingly numerous armies, from small groups of some dozens of individuals to groups of hundreds of soldiers, increasing again in the

Neolithic and throughout the entirety of history. The data gathered by Gat demolishes the theories that were elaborated mainly in the 1960s which depicted human struggle as a cultural phenomenon that developed especially in Europe from the Neolithic period onwards.

Soon, these discoveries led to the theory that fighting had an instinctive character in the human species, in addition to having been an important factor in its technological superiority. Far from what is claimed by postmodern theories—which attribute to man a peaceful and anti-conflictive nature, altered only by a corrupt and pathological Western civilization—the inclination to strive and fight has not been the product of a warmongering cultural narrative but derives instead from a fundamental instinct of man which is present to a greater or lesser extent in all human cultures. The tendency to fight has not been, therefore, an acquired cultural product, but a natural instinct.

David Buss, professor at the University of Texas, believes that the answer to the old debate on nature and cultural influence (nature or nurture), two opposing views adopted to explain human attitudes and behaviors, has been surpassed by the renewed branch of social studies called evolutionary psychology. This scientific discipline affirms that, while the cultural environment can influence certain attitudes and actions, these could not be possible without a biological basis. Hence, no matter how much a person is exposed to violence—for example, through the media or through a warmongering culture—any possible violent reaction would not occur in the absence of a biology designed for that purpose.

Biologists such as the German ethologist and Nobel laureate Konrad Lorenz believed that the ability of humans to fight, compete, and be aggressive was rooted in this physiological element. According to Lorenz, the tendency to fight was the product of a natural instinct regulated by biology. He argued that struggle became part of man's biology; that all of his systems, muscles, and organs adapted to allow him to fight and defend himself in a process of relentless natural selection. Desmond Morris, a renowned English ethologist, described in a remarkable way part of this ever-on-guard mechanism that is physiologically related to fighting and based on the automatic functioning of the nervous system and its two sub-systems: sympathetic and parasympathetic, which are responsible for preparing the body for violent activity.

> When this [the sympathetic system] is activated, adrenalin pours into the blood and the whole circulatory system is profoundly affected. The heart beats faster and blood is transferred from the skin and viscera to the muscles and brain. There is an increase in blood pressure. The rate of production of red blood corpuscles is rapidly stepped up. There is a reduction of the time taken for blood to coagulate. In addition there is a cessation in the processes of digesting and storing food. Salivation is restrained. Movements of the stomach, the secretion of gastric juices, and the peristaltic movements of the intestines are all inhibited. Also, the rectum and bladder do not empty as easily as under normal conditions. Stored carbohydrate is rushed out of the liver and floods the blood with sugar. There is a massive increase in respiratory activity. Breathing becomes quicker and deeper. The temperature-regulating mechanisms are activated. The hair stands on end. . . .[82]

Lorenz believed that struggle was present in nature under various aspects, the most evident being the struggle between species, which fought in the context of the dynamics of the food chain, being hunters and prey at the same time. Struggle also existed between species that did not confront each other in the context of the food chain, but did so when competing for the same food, resources, or living spaces. However, a third type of struggle was intraspecific, meaning it took place among a single species, and in humans within their different groups.

In the human species, intraspecific struggle is commonly called aggression. Aggression also plays an evolutionary role, despite being much less damaging and lethal than fighting against other groups. It rather serves as a mechanism of regulation of status in the

---

[82] Morris, *The Naked Ape*, Chapter 5.

sense of a method of general preservation. A moderate struggle between human groups allows for the rise of leaders who are
beneficial to the community. In line with the theories of Darwin, internal struggles among groups of organisms are caused by a lack of
resources which force the conflicting parties to separate in order to
achieve a better territorial distribution, therefore avoiding a greater
evil, that is, the extinction of the entire group due to the complete
depletion of resources in their habitat.

In addition to the studies of Lorenz and Morris, the progress that
was made in neurological and genetic studies has also led to the discovery of inheritable traits aimed at both offense and defense.
According to the psychiatrist Adrian Raine, it is clear that a genetics
of struggle exists. Sequences such as the MAOA genotype, the 5HTT,
DRD2, DATI, DRD genes, or the genetics responsible for the production of neurotransmitting substances, such as serotonin and
adrenaline, can be linked to a biology that facilitates aggressive and
confrontational responses. These are the so-called "warrior genes,"
inheritable traits that have succeeded in the great struggle for the
existence of mankind. Professor Jim Taylor, Ph.D. at the University
of San Francisco, believes that the process of natural selection which
favors the "warrior genes" is still at work in the modern human being. Emotions that are referred to as "hot," such as surprise, disgust,
and determination, are experienced instantaneously and with intensity. On the other hand, "cold" emotions, such as love and happiness,
are not immediately accessible, requiring much longer periods of
time to consolidate.

Everything mentioned above is the evidence of a long evolutionary process oriented toward the selection of inheritable traits that
allow for an ever-active combat capability, useful for securing resources and fighting for hierarchy, status, access to reproduction,
hunting, and territorial defense. Even when these instincts gradually
became more tempered and moderated by culture, the physiology
of fighting still had to be always present and ready for use. Although
engaging in constant acts of conflict could bring mortal wounds or
gradual impairment, cultivating a warrior reputation—based on the
controlled but effective use of aggression—was fundamental because it minimized the chances of receiving constant external

aggressions. The research in evolutionary psychology has shown that this led to the development of tactical skills that minimized the risks of fighting while still reaping its benefits, a process that resulted in the outburst of rational intelligence which is typical of the human species.

Mind, will, emotions, and psychology, as well as physical capabilities and biological characteristics, are a byproduct of selective processes, which were always geared toward the struggle for existence in the most literal sense of the expression. This physiological evolution created culture and also determined its typology, including ethical and moral codes. As repulsive as it may sound today, the mechanisms of aggressiveness and confrontation allowed for the solution of countless problems of adaptability during the thousands-year-old evolutionary path of man. Ultimately, this instinct is what allowed mankind to continue to exist to this day.

MOTHERS AND WARRIORS

Living in a perpetual struggle for existence throughout hundreds of thousands of years of evolution has not only generated a biology which is fit to this purpose, but also shaped the culture in accordance with these objectives. In these stages of human evolution, nature and culture were inextricably bound together.

In polemological cultures—a term coined by de Benoist that refers to cultures and peoples living under the polemological logic of life as a struggle—there were essentially two major social roles. These originated from the evolution of the human species into two genders, males and females. The successful history of preservation and progress, characteristic of the human species, was achieved by specializing the sexes in the roles of warrior or nurturer of offspring respectively. Thus, men carried out the masculine role of the warrior hero, and women the feminine role of the great mother. Therefore, gender roles were not created because of eccentric cultural impulses, but rather by the ability to rationalize instinctive nature, adapting all vital forces to cultural codes fit for the struggle for existence.

This successful evolutionary path resulted in the long gestation and rearing periods of human females beneficial for the good development of their offspring, which in turn made them unable to take part in other tasks within the community. This prolonged period of maternity was needed because their short average life expectancy of about twenty to thirty years allowed them to conceive only a few children, most of whom would never reach the reproductive age. Evolutionary specialization in fertility and parenting was therefore vitally necessary for the preservation of the species. On the contrary, human males, because of their freedom in the function of conception and breeding, specialized themselves in protecting the community and gathering resources. In addition, due to the limited number of women who were not pregnant or lactating, fierce competition arose among men for reproductive resources, and after intense battles, they submitted to the females' will of choice. Because of this, together with the fact that primitive men were ordinary and common "goods," and in a certain way, expendable—since there were plenty of men available for reproduction—they strengthened their specialization in warfare and other dangerous tasks, consolidating their role as warriors and protectors of the community.

Fights against their male peers and enough free time for hunting and warfare with other groups led men to a selection process that resulted in the development of a biology and psychology typical of warriors. During this process, men obtained genetics geared toward the development of muscle mass in addition to the brain power needed for strategy and problem-solving. At the same time, females were biologically allowed to neglect the development of muscle mass and other functions dedicated to raw strength, replacing these with a finely developed agility and a sharp and intuitive intellectual ability oriented toward establishing emotional ties with family and society, in addition to playing the role of priestesses or intermediaries between the world of humans and the world of the gods.

Melissa M. McDonald, a researcher at the University of California, using the role of the warrior as an example explains how these ancestral gender roles met specific evolutionary objectives which, according to her psychological analysis, remain valid to this day. The evolutionary characteristics which defined gender roles were the result of hundreds of thousands of years of selection. Their modification cannot be the result of a rational decision—let alone a political one—but only the consequence of the creation of new strategies for preservation which are linked to age-old evolutionary changes. McDonald gives an account of the considerable evidence in terms of samples and studies that prove the theory of the male warrior. Males present more accentuated ethnocentric tendencies than females. They are also more capable of detecting external threats and are inclined to dehumanize members of other groups. Therefore, McDonald believes that "the male warrior hypothesis implies that men may be more motivated to support and defend the in-group. This should be particularly true when faced with threats from another group."[83]

---

[83] McDonald, et al, "Evolution and the psychology."

DEFENDING THE BORDER

Human evolution followed a path similar to that of many other species in which males became warriors and protectors of the boundaries of the community, and females became mothers dedicated to the nurturing of the children, a task that did not preclude them by any means from taking up arms in order to defend the community from external attacks. The warrior tradition was truly the first tradition, the only cultural creation that has been with mankind since its beginning. The heroic tradition has therefore been the foundation of the development of society because it originated from man's most primal instinct: the tendency to survive through struggle. In polemological cultures, nature and culture were bound together.

According to Desmond Morris, this was also resulted from the close bond between stable heterosexual couples that mitigated the competition within groups of males for reproduction, establishing a social agreement in which men and women were partners in monogamous and long-lasting relationships. Thus, the warrior energy could be shifted from competition among peers to the protection of the family and community in general.

Morris suggests that this cultural change occurred due to the success of an evolutionary process that prioritized stable relationships through biological mechanisms. Differently from the mating behavior of most species, human reproduction has always been characterized by a significantly intimate contact that greatly strengthened monogamous and heteroparental bonds. Evolutionary processes led the reproductive instinct, which in other animal species is limited exclusively to the period of fertility, to develop into sexuality, that is, into the search for pleasure beyond the mere re-production. Morris' description of the sexual biology of man is surprising. The biological evolution of the human species resulted in the development of male and female erogenous zones and mating indicators in the front part of the body while, in the majority of spe-cies, females have them in the rear part and males in the front part of the body. The human reproductive act evolved biologically so that it could be performed from the front, gazing at the partner. Morris suggests that the frontal relationship also facilitated intimate com-munication during reproduction, allowing the formation of a strong bond between the partners.

Melissa McDonald argues that the creation of cohesive families and clans evolved simultaneously with the instinctive psychological behavior associated with the ability to distinguish and discriminate. This consolidated the creation of actual community armies, leagues of warriors founded on instinctive solidarity between groups with blood kinship and ethnocultural affinities. Thus, the immense intra-group solidarity became proportional to the intense aggressiveness toward the other groups that competed for the scarce resources of the prehistoric age. Indeed, intra-group solidarity brought tremen-dous benefits in terms of survival and reproduction, such as the mutual sharing of resources, specialization of labor, cooperative parenthood, collective protection, and territorial defense. It was the awareness of these benefits that led to an increase in the *positive* valuation of the community and the negative perception of what was outside the group, turning this mechanism of "discrimination" into an integral part of the human psychological structure.

> Yet what may be surprising are the positive and negative af-fective evaluations automatically connected to perceptions of one's own group (*in-group*) versus another group (*out-group*). Such in-group–out-group biases have been docu-mented widely among both Western and non-Western populations. . . . The automatic tendency to favour members of one's own group at the expense of members of out-groups, referred to here as tribalism or parochialism, might simply be

a by-product of generic cognitive adaptations for classifying the physical world around us.[84]

Despite all of this, the sacrifice of the warriors for the preservation of the group has been questioned by a whole anthropological school of thought, which considers it improbable and in contradiction with the survival instinct. This school has tried to atomize the fighting instinct by attributing an individualistic aim to it. Libertarian and anarcho-capitalist political theories have emerged from this line of thought. But this way of understanding the phenomenon clashes with the other scientific tradition that considered polemological instincts a way of preserving human groups and not the single individual.

Moreover, researchers such as Richard Dawkins, an evolutionary biologist at Oxford University, claim that biological preservation does not aim at safeguarding individual biological organisms, but their genes. According to his theory of the "Selfish Gene," hereditary characteristics are the most important factors that must be preserved, and they are not the exclusive heritage of particular individuals, but of groups. Dawkins explains how the altruistic sacrifice of the individual benefits the larger group, which bears the same genetic characteristics:

> What is a single selfish gene trying to do? It is trying to get more numerous in the gene pool. Basically it does this by helping to program the bodies in which it finds itself to survive and to reproduce. . . . [A] gene might be able to assist *replicas* of itself that are sitting in other bodies. . . . If an individual dies in order to save ten close relatives, one copy of the kin-altruism gene may be lost, but a larger number of copies of the same gene is saved.[85]

---

[84] Ibid.
[85] Dawkins, *The Selfish Gene*, Chapter 6.

The so-called "selfish gene" is what induces the solidarity of parents with their own offspring, between relatives, and among communities that are perceived as peers.

Frank Salter, an Australian political scientist, believes that the ability to perceive the phenotypical similarity of human groups or the certainty of a common ancestry are identity factors that awaken instincts of group solidarity and cohesion in order to act against other competing groups. Evidence also indicates that these behaviors have proven to be successful strategies for adaptation, resource acquisition, and preservation. Irenaus Eibl-Eibesfeldt, zoologist at the University of Munich, maintained that ethnocultural solidarity is based on the "genetic interest" for preservation, a mechanism which works just as family relationships do. This was also supported by the Canadian psychologist J. Philippe Rushton, who elaborated the theory of "Genetic Similarity." According to his analysis, ethnic solidarity increases the capabilities of genes shared by members of a community. Rushton provided interesting statistics, demonstrating how in Western societies the majority of people prefer ethnically and culturally similar partners and friends. Due to this tendency, genetic studies on current populations, as well as on ancient human remains, have been able to establish a surprising age-old continuity of genetic lineages (haplogroups) and ethnic groups, both patrilineal and matrilineal, thus confirming the cultural and evolutionary atavism of maintaining cohesive and blood-related human groups and identities as a way of distinguishing who to protect and who to confront.

Pierre L. van den Berghe, professor emeritus of sociology and anthropology at the University of Washington, argued that biological solidarity is a far more powerful instinct than nationality. Trust between those who are similar to each other is essential for joining forces in the struggle for preservation. According to Van den Berghe, just as armies identify themselves by providing "uniforms" to their troops, group behaviors are based on identity and similarity when it comes to joint efforts. "[T]here is abundant evidence that natural se-lection favored nepotistic organisms, because, by favoring kin, organisms are contributing to their own inclusive fitness."[86]

---

[86] Van den Berghe, *The Ethnic Phenomenon*, 239.

BIRTH OF THE MYTH

In the opinion of the French anthropologist Jacques de Mahieu, the biology of man, his physiology and biochemistry, have been gradually able to create more and more complex mental images. It is the so-called cenesthetic sensation, the perception of one's own corporeality through mental, psychological, and spiritual experience. This resulted in a feeling of existence through which human consciousness became aware of the sensory experience of the body and its instincts. This same conscious cenesthetic experience applies also to external stimuli, to the images of the world. It is for this reason that the reactions to the threats of the environment, and the dynamics and forces of nature, ceased to be solely instinctive and became conscious as well. Thus, consciousness became capable of "arranging" the mental images that it received from external and internal perception. With this, a dualism of consciousness did not emerge, but rather the "instinctive consciousness" and the "rational consciousness" worked together in a unified psyche. Ultimately, both the instinctive consciousness and the rational consciousness provided images of psychological, or rather biopsychic character, as de Mahieu termed it.

Nevertheless, human evolution separated instincts from reason in modes of action, or rather it created a mechanism of double analysis, an instinctive one followed by a rational one. The difference was, as de Mahieu argued, that the former could not reflect on its actions, while the latter had the ability to choose. Thus, human evolution created a psyche that could function in an automatic way but at the same time could be judicious in taking certain actions. This was necessary to make the leap toward rationality without neglecting instinct, since cells, organs, and instinctive attitudes would collapse if they questioned their objectives by means of theories or by the "mental" flights of some sort of rational consciousness at the organic level. However, mental rationality holds the ability to judge and evaluate in order to direct its will. As de Mahieu explained, this ability of double analysis was developed to improve the individual's capability to assert his own lifespan, although the professor did not fail to notice and to regret that historical evolution has, in the end, separated these two complementary functions into the so-called dualism of body and soul, the division between biology and consciousness, between nature and spirit. According to de Mahieu, man buried his instinctive attitudes, or rather the images induced in his psyche by these instinctive attitudes, to replace them with a rational, organized, understandable, and transmissible structure. Myths and legends, ancestral traditions, and social customs were ways of regulating instincts and understanding the world and the role played by man and community in the cosmos.

Thus primitive people, thanks to the secondary ability of mental analysis, were able to gain awareness of their environment and its dynamic, ever-changing, and threatening nature. This was the way by which they were able to integrate into the environment, identifying themselves with these forces and recognizing them in their own psyche, and creating a morality and vision of the world that embraced the laws of nature, assigning to these natural forces mythical representations: the "Gods." This is how the struggle for life, the warrior instinct, the reproductive instinct, and the care for the clan, among other aspects, were enveloped in a poetic and mythical cultural veil in order to transmit social behaviors aimed at the preservation and progress of civilization. Later on, as rational thought developed more and more, these systems of values based on mythology evolved into philosophies, civil codes, and complex religious cults.

In the opinion of de Mahieu, the doctrine that considers the myth a primitive predecessor of logical thought was false. Myths originated from the rationalized thought that allowed us to organize the chaotic forces of nature—which were also at work within the human mind itself—in order to understand and make use of them. In other words, myths, gods, and legends would not have been a way of bowing down to an anxious lack of understanding of the natural environment and its dynamics, but on the contrary would have been the means by which those chaotic natural dynamics were organized and systematized. The transformation of the instincts and forces of nature into gods and totems would have been thoughtful and rational, and the transmission of these ideas and images through myths and legends was a way of passing them on to the less privileged strata of the community, those without the creative and rational capacity to understand the eternally mysterious forces of the universe and the nature of man.

THE AGE OF THE GODS

The most distant echo of the cultural concept of life as a struggle comes from the myths and legends of the mysterious Proto-Indo-European culture. This term refers to the cultural and historical period during which the various Indo-European peoples lived in a common homeland, approximately around the 5th millennium BC. Later on, during the Iron Age, these populations migrated and split into the communities that reached from the Indus Valley to the entirety of Europe. These groups were the founders of the Greek, Roman, Germanic, Celtic, Aryan, and Persian cultures, among others.

The confirmation of the existence of a common culture to all peoples has its scientific basis in cultural and linguistic similarities. All Indo-European peoples had their roots in a common Proto-Indo-European culture and language. The worldview that these peoples had before developing this culture—during the times of the North Eurasian populations of hunter-gatherers—is unclear and out of reach.

Comparative studies in linguistics, archaeology, mythology, and genetics—along with the revelatory studies on the Indo-European genetic lineages called haplogroups R1a and R1b—have provided us with a sufficiently detailed portrait of what this ancient society may have been like. The reconstruction of primitive words carried out by M. L. West, a researcher at Oxford University, revealed the existence of precise geographic locations, customs, social contracts, human relationships, social stratifications, and several other characteristics. Generally speaking, Proto-Indo-European culture appears to be that of a society which flourished 7,000 years ago. The characteristics that have been discovered reveal a Neolithic society that domesticated horses and other animals, practiced cereal agriculture, inhabited a geographic location with a cold climate and frequent

snow, had knowledge of the wheel and navigation, forged sophisti-
cated weapons, built chariots for transport and combat, and also
worshipped warrior gods and wrote heroic poetry.

The reconstruction of the Proto-Indo-European language also
gives us an idea of the abstract character of their thought. One of the
most important words that can help to understand the Proto-Indo-
European culture is *Ar*, which probably meant "to shape," "to unite,"
"to bring together," or "to come into being." The word *Ar* has several
variants such as *Haer*, *Artus*, and *Xertus*, which are also the roots of
the words art, rite, and of the Latin words *ordo* and *ratio*. To come
into being, to be something, meant in the Indo-European culture to
shine, to take shape and to separate oneself from the ordinary, and
to succeed in giving order to chaos, which remarkably reminds us of
the Heideggerian "clearing." Mankind, culture, art, order, and ethics
were all *Ar*, *Artus* or *Xertus*. Indo-European mythology depicted *Ar*
as a rod, tree, or mountain in the center of a patch of land surrounded by water. This myth was brought along with every Indo-
European migration.

The myths of Proto-Indo-European culture described the universe, or rather the structure of the universe, as shapeless chaos, an
undifferentiated, unified mass of nothingness. Amid the chaos—represented by waters, dragons, or serpents—a portion of dry land
appeared, an island, an analogy of what is concrete and certain. According to ancient legends, the island, the patch of land, was created
by the god *Manus*, by sacrificing the Proto-Indo-European deity
Yemos. With the skull of *Yemos*, *Manus* created the sky; with his
limbs, the earth; and with his blood, the rivers. This legend of the
creation of the world through the partition of a primordial Being,
with some variations, can be found in all Indo-European mythologies and is probably an analogy for struggle as the means of
preserving the particularity of human life against the inevitable dissolution into the undifferentiated mass of earth from which it
emerged.

The sacrificial rite of *Yemos* was the analogy of the instant during
which the undifferentiated "One"—the chaos, the water—was transformed into the "multitude"—the concrete, the variety of shapes of
the entities of the world. By the sword of the sacrifice that split and

separated into differentiated parts, order arrived, and the entities became distinct and recognizable, losing their undifferentiated nature, symbolized by the water. Nevertheless, the myth was quite clear: chaos was never defeated; indeed chaos was actually necessary as it was a part of order. In Indo-European mythologies there was no dualism, but rather a polarity or a binomial relationship, the synergetic coexistence of order and chaos.

On the soil of the island surrounded by water grew the tree, the rod that produced the fruits of abundance. And although the tree grew on dry land, it also sank its roots deep into the waters of chaos. *Ar* or *Xartus* was order created from raw chaos. Without chaos there would be nothing to be put in order, and without order there would be no *Artus* and nothing and nobody could take shape. To the question of why there are beings and not nothingness, the answer during Proto-Indo-European times was very clear: because of *Ar* and his ability to raise the sword and divide the "One" in order to transform it into a multitude, to create plots of dry land in the middle of the waters. The similarities between Indo-European mythology and Heideggerian thought are striking.

The act of sacrifice was the duty of the hero. In Indo-European mythologies there is always present a story of a hero who fights against a dragon or serpent. This was an analogy of the process of taking over ground from chaos and nothingness in order to bring into being, and preserve, the diversity of the entities of the world, including, of course, man. For this reason, the hero undertook the task of giving order to chaos, of stabilizing the becoming, even though he knew perfectly well that his struggle would never manage to prevail over the waters of indefiniteness, since those were essentially the fundamental element of his own action. What was heroic in the actions of the warrior was precisely the fatality of giving order to chaos, knowing that nature was not static. Therefore, victory was achieved by delaying temporarily the becoming. The warrior did not strive to mummify everything, to establish everlasting archetypes or eternal truths. The warrior loved change because it allowed for struggle, and it represented new perspectives and new paths to travel by means of will. Paving a path, defining one's own life, and creating something new were all heroic ideals. Life as a struggle was motion and action. Nietzsche claimed that the warrior had the ability to briefly settle reality according to his will, forcing things to become as he commanded.

The heroic culture of the Indo-European peoples was a reflection of this myth of the creation of the universe. The warrior was the one who established order through his will to power, allowing for the survival of human existence. Through the ability to fight and his sacrifice to the blade, man kept the waters of chaos at bay. Through struggle man created boundaries and distinctions allowing for the existence of concrete entities, families, and nations. Without struggle, the becoming would defeat man; entities would lose their shape, culture would decay, and peoples would disappear. A culture without struggle was inconceivable for the Indo-European peoples and the whole of their culture and tradition was a reflection of this core value.

As Indo-European migrations reached the most distant corners of the globe, these ideas and myths diversified. Also, with time, logical thought transformed myth into philosophy, scientific thought, and organic tradition. In this regard, the most comprehensive warrior tradition that has been transmitted to us comes from ancient Greece. While there are written fragments belonging to other peoples related to the Greeks—other members of the so-called great Indo-European family—these were often excessively poetic during the mythological phase, as well as fragmented or later, and affected by the contamination of cultural syncretism. In addition, there is not another people of ancient times that embraced in such a complete way the concept of life as a struggle. Although many other warrior peoples existed, only the Greeks developed such a rich and noble agonal culture, and one of the most important preclassical Greek thinkers among those who conceived the idea of life as a struggle was Heraclitus of Ephesus.

DIVERSIFICATION OF POLEMOS

In the opinion of Alfred Bäumler, the Heraclitean worldview put Polemos and conflict in charge of delivering justice in the world. Life as a struggle made it possible for entities to rise and preserve themselves depending on their possibilities and abilities. Polemos was the father of all things, and also the ruler, two functions closely related to justice in the Indo-European world.

The connection existing within the pre-Socratic Greek culture between conflict, government, and justice, understood as expressions of a heroic worldview, had many correlations and variations in other cultural areas of Proto-Indo-European origin. Even in the Greek peninsula, Polemos shared functions and characteristics with the god of war Ares and the goddess of conflict Eris. Subsequently, the Roman civilization adopted this tradition in the form of cults and legends surrounding Mars, the Roman god of war, and Discordia, the goddess of conflict. Bellona, the wife of Mars, also showed the characteristics of a warrior. Even Zeus, as the father of the Greek gods, and Jupiter, father of the Roman gods, have inherited part of the characteristics of Polemos. Polemos, later in time, diversified itself further and it is possible to find it in all the Greco-Latin culture and in that of the other Indo-European peoples.

Georges Dumezil, French philologist and historian, compellingly argued that the diversification of divine functions led to different gods and heroes sharing and exchanging characteristics. What is important about this diversification is to understand the themes and cultural foundations replicated and shared among the great Indo-European family. Through comparative mythology it is possible to extract a cultural foundation and a tradition.

In this regard, the Norse cultural universe presents the most intriguing and closest connections to the Greek worldview. Unfortunately, all information concerning these myths and cultures has come to us only by late medieval sources.

In Norse mythology, the greatest heir to the original worldview was probably the god of war, Tyr. In Dumezil's view, Tyr served the role of god of war and justice. Etymologically, his name also indicated the roles of father and ruler. The name Tyr derived from the ancient *Tiwas*, etymological successor of the Indo-European *Dieus*. Therefore, he shared its roots with the name of Zeus (*Deus*) and Jupiter (*Dius pater*, father god), as well as with the *Dievas* of Baltic mythology and the *Diaus Pita* found in the Vedas, among others. The very name of God today is the continuation of this tradition.

There is not much else that we know about Tyr. Jackson Crawford, professor of Old Norse and expert in Scandinavian mythology, explains that Tyr is associated with war because of a poem (*Lokasenna*) in which Loki, a dark mythological deity, calls him "someone who does not makes peace, but instead enjoys affronting, or setting two people against each other." According to Dumezil, Tyr was the oldest and most important god of the Nordic people, only becoming superseded by Odin (Wotan) in much later times, perhaps due to the supremacy of some Germanic tribe especially devoted to Odin rather than to Tyr. In this regard, Cornelius Tacitus, the Roman historian who lived during the first century of our era, in his book "Germania" pointed out that the most ancient god of the Germanic tribes was *Tuisto*, a name that some contemporary researchers etymologically link to Tyr. Tacitus used "Mars," the Roman god of war, to translate the Germanic mythology to his Latin readers. The other gods mentioned by Tacitus were Mercury, in an allusion to Odin; Hercules, assumed to represent Thor; and Isis, who probably coincided with Freya. Another proof of the supremacy of Tyr in antiquity is the toponymy bearing etymological roots derived from his name. This toponymy is quite widespread, proving a popularity which is more ancient in relation to Odin—the supreme god according to late sources such as the Edda of the tenth century—whose toponymy concentrates in what would be his place of origin.

On this matter, Dumezil warned that the cult of the warrior god Tyr, deliverer of justice and father of all things, was not suppressed or replaced by Odin/Wotan. Perhaps it is fairer to say that the whole warrior tradition of Odin, god of the raging horde, was the product of variants that continued the most ancient cults of Tyr, adapted to new historical and geographical circumstances. Heinrich Niedner, a Danish philosopher specialized in Norse mythology, provided a description of Odin that brings to mind polemological functions quite clearly, thereby supporting Dumezil's thesis. In the end Odin, Wotan, Mars, Ares, Tyr, and Polemos were a single mythological concept, sometimes covering more roles and sometimes less, according to the specific needs of the cultures that developed them. Odin's characteristics as the father of all things, the chief of warriors, as well as the ruler and deliverer of justice, creator of science and poetry, and as the spirit of life were all ones that he shared with Polemos.

THE HEROIC AGE

Greek myths and pre-Socratic philosophy were the expression of a naturalistic view of life. Within this, man and the gods were part of the universal order and as such they fought like any other being. The age of myths and legends of the warrior gods laid the foundations for the age of heroes, a Greek cultural stage during which human consciousness regulated its fighting instinct in accordance with a culture with solid and well-structured warrior codes. During the Heroic Age, Polemos took a distinctly militaristic aspect.

The Heroic Age can be framed in the period of time that began with the arrival of the Indo-European peoples into the Greek peninsula in the fourteenth century BC. The Heroic Age saw the most famous of conflicts, the Trojan War, a saga of heroes and warriors that probably occurred in the eleventh century BC, sung by Homer during the twilight of that era. Nietzsche believed that the most authentic expression of Greek culture was to be found in the Heroic Age, the cultural phase in which the heroic poems, especially those of Homer, were the ethical standard of a people that made of fighting a value in itself. According to Nietzsche, after the end of this Age, the appearance of metaphysics and Orphic cults would lead Greece to lose all of its greatness.

In this culture those who excelled as warriors were the most virtuous and outstanding. Their exceptional nature made them aristocratic, a term derived from *aristos*, the bearers of the *arete*: the excellence. The search for virtue and exceptionality was analogous to the selective processes found in nature, since natural order seeks the preservation of the community through exceptional individuals. It is for this reason that the Greek hero did not enjoy the benefits of the *arete* in an individualistic way, as prominent people do today.

The Greek hero fulfilled a communitarian pedagogical function. The dream of every Greek was not only to achieve fame, but to be recognized as an example for the community to follow. In the opinion of Nietzsche, the warrior based his actions on "serving the State beneath the shade of the gods." In the case of committing an unworthy deed, inappropriate to his honor, he felt social shame, but never guilt. The rewards received by the heroes were not material, and certainly not inheritable. His ultimate reward was to be the bearer of excellence and, therefore, to have honor. Honor was exclusive, individual, and hierarchical. It was not an egalitarian value, nor social, nor could it be delegated to a specific representative position. It was only earned in battle and its worth was determined in relation to who the opponent was, how the battle was fought, and how it was won. The heroic path showed how human will was greater than external events. Therefore, the hero was willing to risk his life to achieve his goals and reach excellence.

This polemological foundation permeated the entire history of the West. American military historian Victor Davis Hanson believes that, since ancient Greece onwards, the Indo-European tradition—be it Roman, Celtic, Viking, or ultimately Western—has been by far superior in warfare to any other culture. There is no other culture in which the heroic archetype was so widespread and influential. There is no other culture that committed more time and resources to war tactics, as well as to the production and technological development of weaponry and devices intended for warfare and defense.

THE GOOD ERIS

James Whitley, an archaeologist at Cardiff University, believes that toward the end of the Heroic Age, around the seventh century BC, the archetype of the hero as a pedagogical figure of Greek culture began to become increasingly difficult to find. This led to the deification of the ancient Homeric warrior. Heracles, the Dioscuri, Achilles, Agamemnon, Helen, Odysseus, and Theseus, among hundreds of other heroes, became part of a renewed Greek pantheon in a culture that felt a sense of inferiority due to the lack of heroic activity during its period.

The stage of stabilization following the Indo-European conquests left room for the creation of cultural products of a less warlike character than those produced during the Heroic Age. During this era, Polemos showed its kind side. The spirit of striving for excellence and *arete*, the thirst for eternal self-improvement and struggle against adversity, was shifted from the battlefield to civilian life. Games, competitions, politics, and every other activity of the various Hellenic cities were enveloped in a true agonal spirit derived from the warrior will of the previous centuries. This inclination for competition and fighting within civilian life was understood as the other side of the goddess of war Eris, a goddess that matched the Heraclitean Polemos. The good Eris, unlike the bad Eris, exercised the power of conflict for the creation of culture and progress.

The division of struggle and conflict into positive and negative aspects was devised by Hesiod, a poet from the seventh century BC, in his popular works of poetry. In his hymn to the Olympian gods and legends, the *Theogony,* he depicted the warmongering and destructive Eris, and in his poem *Works and Days* her positive counterpart appears, the good and creative Eris. And, although Hesiod suggests that they are ultimately two aspects of the same goddess, their contrasts are evident. The evil Eris was described by Hesiod as a cold-hearted divinity responsible for driving man to conflict and war. The second Eris, on the other hand, was described as the cause of the struggle that allowed for the fulfillment and progress of man through work:

> So, after all, there was not one kind of Strife alone, but all over the earth there are two. As for the one, a man would praise her when he came to understand her; but the other is blameworthy: and they are wholly different in nature. For one fosters evil war and battle, being cruel: her no man loves; but perforce, through the will of the deathless gods, men pay harsh Strife her honour due. But the other is the elder daughter of dark Night, and the son of Cronos who sits above and dwells in the aether, set her in the roots of the earth: and she is far kinder to men. She stirs up even the shiftless to toil.[87]

Professor Jonathan Zarecki has pointed out that both of Hesiod's Erises have their place in life, specifically the struggle in war and the struggle in the field—two sisters who balanced each other in equilibrium. According to Hesiod, one had first to take advantage of the good Eris by working the land, toiling, and striving for excellence in everyday life. Only then could one follow the evil Eris, and engage in war and seek the path that led to the gods and to the glory of the victorious hero.

However, the division of the two Eris should not be confused with the dualism that was later introduced in Greek culture by Socrates. Dualism deemed the essence of the opposites distinct and irreconcilable, meaning that they excluded each other, thus tending toward bringing discord in the world. And although Hesiod believed that one Eris deserved disapproval and the other praise, Nietzsche pointed out that the good and the evil Eris complemented each

---

[87] Hesiod, *Hesiod*, 3.

other, being an integral part of a single concept, of life as a struggle, of the order of the world established by the immortal gods.

Indeed, Nietzsche took into consideration the phrase written on a metallic sheet of the oldest copy of *Works and Days*, where it was stated that "two Eris goddesses are on earth," affirming that this is "one of the most remarkable Hellenic thoughts and worth inscribing for all who come before the entrance gate to Greek ethics."[88] This was a cultural principle that saw conflict as a force that could be negative, yet not negative in itself, because it could be transformed into a positive one, or at least into an ontological foundation since it was placed on earth by "high-ruling Zeus." [89] Eris, the goddess of discord—similarly to Polemos—was understood, according to Nietzsche, as a universal force which stimulated work, even if by the desire to surpass one's neighbor because of zeal, resentment, or envy, or the desire to win in competitions. All these were instincts driven by confrontation, which if used well could nevertheless be beneficial to the community.

> However, the greater and more sublime a Greek is, the brighter the ambitious flame breaks out of him, consuming everyone who runs with him on the same path. . . . There was no ambition toward the unmeasured and immeasurable as modern ambition generally is: the youth thought of the well-being of his native city when he sang or threw or ran in contests; he wished to increase the city's share of glory by increasing his own glory; to his city's gods he dedicated the wreaths that the judges placed upon his head in honor. Every Greek felt in himself, from childhood on, the burning wish to be an instrument of the well-being of his city in the contest of the cities: with this his selfishness was enflamed, with this it was bridled and restrained.[90]

Heraclitean thought greatly influenced Nietzsche. The German philosopher found in the pre-classical or pre-Socratic Greek tradition

---

[88] Nietzsche, *Homer's Contest*, 3.
[89] Ibid., 3.
[90] Ibid., 4, 5–6.

the first and clearest traces of the original concept of life as a struggle upon which his vitalist and hierarchical doctrine was based:

> It is a wonderful idea, welling up from the purest strings of Hellenism, the idea that strife embodies the everlasting sovereignty of strict justice, bound to everlasting laws. Only a Greek was capable of finding such an idea to be the fundament of a cosmology; it is Hesiod's good *Eris* transformed into the cosmic principle; it is the contest-idea of the Greek individual and the Greek state, taken from the gymnasium and the palaestra, from the artist's *agon*, from the contest between political parties and between cities—all transformed into universal application so that now the wheels of the cosmos tum on it.[91]

It is not a coincidence, then, to find Heraclitus among Nietzsche's most relevant influences. "*Heraclitus*, in whose vicinity I feel altogether warmer, better disposed than anywhere else. The affirmation of transience *and destruction*, the decisive feature of any Dionysian philosophy, saying 'yes' to opposition and war."[92]

Nietzsche believed that there was no dualism in Polemos and that the forces in conflict were eternally in struggle, without a final synthesis or a teleological end; without eternal opposites, there was only perpetual struggle as an agonal game of essentially equivalent forces, engaged in the eternal dance of combat and the creation of shapes and forms.

> The strife of the opposites gives birth to all that comes-to-be; the definite qualities which look permanent to us express but the momentary ascendency of one partner. But this by no means signifies the end of the war; the contest endures in all eternity. Everything that happens, happens in accordance

---

[91] Nietzsche, *Philosophy in the Tragic Age*, 55.
[92] Nietzsche, *Ecce Homo*, 47–48.

with this strife, and it is just in the strife that eternal justice is revealed.[93]

---

[93] Nietzsche, *Philosophy in the Tragic Age*, 55.

THE SHIELD OF ACHILLES

In Book XVIII of the Iliad, it is possible to find the description of the shield that Hephaestus made for Achilles at the request of his mother Thetis. These lines narrate in great detail what could be considered a fundamental piece of the original inception of the Indo-European people.

In the center of the shield there was depicted the myth of the patch of land surrounded by the undifferentiated waters. The island forged in the center of the shield had the entire universe represented on it. Outside of the inner circle, but still within the patch of land, there was a second layer divided in two parts. Each part represented a city. In the first one scenes of everyday life were portrayed, such as marriages, quarrels, confrontations, lawsuits, trials, and political and communal life. In the other city, the scenes represented were of war, destruction, and military strategies. In the third layer, scenes of hard and unremitting work were depicted, with a section dedicated to the reaping of the crops, another to the grape harvest, and a last one to the shepherding of the cattle. A fourth layer was again divided into three sections, in which were shown the raising of livestock, dances, and the herdsmen with their sheep.

Jessica Wolfe in her book *Homer and the Mythography of Strife* gives an account of a long tradition that interpreted the shield of Achilles as the representation of two equal parts of the same principle: conflict. According to Wolfe, the scenes of the city in peace—or engaged in civil, not military, conflicts—have been arranged in such a way as to either precede or continue the scenes of war. No moral supremacy of any of the two situations exists here, but rather a correlation, a space shared between the two. Conflicts during wars, as

well as during periods of peace, were understood as inevitable situations which were equally part of life on earth, actions that ennobled
man in the same way. Both cities showed the exercise of moral values and political virtues. The good Eris portrayed in legal confrontations and arguments between merchants corresponded to
military strategies, assaults, and the capture of fortifications. Along
the edge of the shield was pictured the arduous life of the workers,
the efforts to harvest, and the struggle to obtain bread and wine
from the earth. Wolfe believes that the legal disputes represented in
the Agora and the clashes of war were the embodiment of a healthy
and flourishing society. Religious and joyful scenes, celebrations,
work, war, and social life—featured not only in the description of
the shield but throughout the Iliad and the Odyssey—danced with
the same intensity on the island which was stolen from the kingdom
of waters of the god Oceanus.

> Engendering "in one same air elation and agony," war in Ho-
> meric epic is fraught with contradiction and paradox. In both
> poems, conflict (*neikos*) is referred to repeatedly as *ho-
> moion*—common, shared, or unifying. For Renaissance
> readers, the epithet strengthens Homer's perceived affinities
> with the cosmology of the pre-Socratic Heraclitus, who holds
> that contraries are "set continually at variance" in a dynamic
> process that Nietzsche would later compare to a struggle be-
> tween "two wrestlers of whom sometimes the one succeeds,
> sometimes the other." In the Iliad, the concept of *neikos ho-
> moiion* and of related epithets such as *xunos Ennualios*
> suggests a counterbalance between opposing armies as well
> as between the adversarial forces of nature in order to convey
> how various forms of strife are governed by *dike*, or distribu-
> tive justice.... Heraclitus reads them as shorthand for the
> eristic processes of his natural philosophy, a philosophy that,
> as Aristotle explains in the Nicomachean Ethics, is founded
> upon the principle of *concordia discors*: "opposition brings

things together . . . and from tones at variance comes beautiful harmony, and all things come to pass through strife."[94]

---

[94] Wolfe, *Homer and the Question*, 32.

THE AGONAL ERA

Jacob Burckhardt, a Swiss historian and friend of Nietzsche, referred to the period following the Indo-European invasions and conquests as the Agonal Age. *Agon* was the term used by the Greeks to define everything that was based on competition and confrontation but did not involve the physical destruction of the opponent. During this era, Polemos transformed itself into competition, the creative confrontation of the good Eris. In agonal Greece—differently from other societies sufficiently advanced to be able to dedicate significant time to art or games—these cultural expressions, and in general any aspect of civil life, were open to all citizens who aspired to excellence and the pursuit of self-improvement. It was this accessible and communitarian character that allowed for the complete integration of the Agon into cultural life. In Greece the agonal contest was democratic, without restrictions of rank, unlike in Egypt, where it was an exclusive activity of the nobles.

During this period the conflict based on competition and victory in the sport, free of any hostility, was at its highest level of expression:

We see it in the conversations and round-songs of the guests in the symposium, in philosophy and legal procedure, down to cock- and quail-fighting or the gargantuan feats of eating. . . . While the agon soon gained ground and indeed became the paramount feature of life, gymnastics were both an alternative and, as we have seen, an offshoot of the agon. The one is unthinkable without the other . . . without the agon, gymnastics could never have become such a distinctive feature of the Hellenes' life. Competitive games were instituted everywhere, even in the smallest communities; the full development of the individual depended on his constantly measuring himself against others in exercises devoid of any direct practical use.... The gymnasium was the chief social centre of Greek life.... As well as this athletic training there was the agon with horses. Because chariot fighting was the noblest form of combat in Homer's war of the heroes, the chariot race was very early ranked highest of all competitions in time of peace.[95]

The Agon was perhaps the most common cultural background in the Hellenic civilization. The entire Greek culture was dominated by the custom of competition, as Burckhardt claimed. It was confrontation in its most profound sense, more than communitarian and never individualistic. In contrast modern competition, as Burckhardt explained, is determined by "quite different aims," since it generally comes from "a few unusually ambitious types," individuals who have replaced the agonal ethic with "something very remote from it, which is business competition."[96]

Among all types of Greek public competitions, the most popular was agonal wrestling in the Olympic arenas. In these competitions, the athletes assumed the same role that ancient warrior heroes fulfilled in the phase of migration and conquest. In this regard, the odes of Pindar that celebrated the glories of the athletes replaced or complemented the ancient warrior poems. In these Olympic odes we find the values of the warrior code, passed on to the agonal competition.

According to American professors Janet Lungstrum and Elizabeth Sauer, the way ancient Greek culture embraced the agonal essence of nature was unparalleled. Greek agonal culture built a society on a foundation that did not disavow natural laws and perfectly blended instinct with spirit, the biological needs that are prone to conflict with the mental abstraction that allowed for the creation of culture.

---

[95] Burckhardt, *The Greeks and Greek Civilization*, 166–168.
[96] Ibid., 183–184.

[N]o other culture in the history of the West has so intertextually defined itself as agonal as did that of the ancient Greeks.... What is amazing about the Greeks' agonistic understanding is that through it they created a society that was "at once nature and culture."[97]

The philosopher Benjamin C. Sax claimed that "the Greeks never considered culture as the opposite of nature," explaining rather that:

[T]hrough the agon they directed violence into positive action, and formed a culture that did not separate nature from culture.... Good Eris contends with bad Eris, but this contention is not a relation of opposites, a dialectical opposition.[98]

Plutarch, a Roman historian who lived in the first century AD, attributed the love of competition to many of the great men of Greco-Roman history, a love without which they would not have been able to achieve glory and the aggrandizement of their people. This agonal and combative spirit, true to the natural essence of man but simultaneously flexible enough to adapt to the abstract needs of a creative and Faustian spirit in search of progress and prosperity, became known as *philoneikia*, or love of strife, of competition, and of struggle.

---

[97] Lungstrum and Sauer, *Agonistics*, 7–8.
[98] Ibid., 57–58.

THE DUALISTIC ERA

Around the sixth century BC, a process of syncretism with East-ern cultures took place in Greece. During this period Polemos, Eris, and the Agon ceased to be the vital substrate from which the spir-itual and cultural products of the Hellenic peninsula emerged. From Africa and the Middle East came a new cultural foundation, the so-called dualism. Introduced in the Hellenic world by Socrates and later by Plato—who was initiated in the mysteries of Egypt—the new dualist culture turned its back on the laws of nature, thus ena-bling the abstractions of the thought to elaborate new normative myths. The entire post-Platonic Indo-European culture can be de-scribed as the fusion of the heroic and agonal Greek culture with the dualistic one that was brought from the Orient. This syncretism has been the cultural and spiritual cornerstone for the development of the West, a culture that continually displays alternating features of these two main cultural sources. These are the two souls of the West, as Oswald Spengler referred to them: the Faustian spirit (Indo-Eu-ropean), and the mystic spirit (Oriental).

In Platonic philosophy the natural and physical world was dual-istically opposed to the world of ideas. The former was a world where things were in a constant state of becoming and struggle. The latter was inhabited by universal and unchanging manifestations. Plato believed, in accordance with Oriental models, in the existence of a world where there was no struggle and from which the soul came before being incarnated on earth. Once the union of the astral soul with the earthly body took place, the latter obtained a warped vision of the perennial forms, achieving a blurred and partial gno-seological understanding of the true nature of the beings. According to Heidegger, the Platonic world of ideas and the world of natural

111

laws were irreconcilable, distinct in their essence and separated by an unbridgeable partition. "Only with the sophists and Plato . . . Being as *idea* was elevated to a supersensory realm. The chasm . . . was torn open between the merely apparent beings here below and the real Being somewhere up there."[99] The Platonic myths meant the end of conflict being part of the essence of man.

The new truth from that moment on became the ideal, that which was external to nature. In this myth, man, the world, and struggle became only illusory shadows of that which is real. The father of all things was from that moment on regarded as a transmundane entity, perfect, devoid of flaws, and invincible. The essence of beings was transformed into an ideal, an eternal and moral archetype, that which is good and perfect in itself. The metaphysical essence was conceived as immobile, unchanging, and incapable of struggle; a conservative entity, mostly unreachable, as well as transcendent, otherworldly, and unfit for man.

Lungstrum and Sauer explained that these new cultural concepts allowed for the development of abstractions of thought that deviated from the laws of life. Thus, the concept of life as a struggle was deemed a punishment, contrasting with the real world:

> Through Plato's rational form of play, the prerational agon was internalized and weakened from its former state of exteriorized social value. As Nietzsche mythically stages it in *The Birth of Tragedy* (1872), the agonal congeniality of the Dionysian and Apollonian art drives was subsumed by the Socratic. In Hellenistic Greek thought, mankind was increasingly separated from its instincts, which came to be depicted as "evil" in relation to the Christian "good": in short, a process began that made the agon into something wholly negative (literally: antagonistic) rather than something life-affirming through the organic cycle of creation and destruction. Expressions of power began to get a bad name, so to speak.[100]

---

[99] Heidegger, *Introduction to Metaphysics*, 111.
[100] Lungstrum and Sauer, *Agonistics*, 9.

In the course of the abandonment of Polemos as an ontological foundation, Greek culture was transformed into a cultural syncretism that gave greater value and moral importance to all that is transmundane, thus not valuing anything that came from nature. But the great beyond was not subject to the recognition of the senses. Rather, it could be approached through altered states of consciousness, magic, and mysticism. Thus, the ancient cults of heroes, which had served as cultural guidance for the development of the agonal ideal, were replaced by a kind of mysticism that strove to penetrate the secrets of the supernatural rather than to understand the dynamics of the natural world. English researcher Lewin Richard Farnell believed that these new metaphysical cults ultimately ended up being administrated in the 5th and 4th centuries BC by a new social class: the priests. So, the mysteries of Eleusis, Bacchus, and more importantly, Orpheus, radically transformed the commemoration of the ancient heroes into authentic dualistic cults. The new Orphic religion, which Farnell linked to the influence of Platonism, placed on the physical body an evil connotation, defining it as a "prison-house or grave of the soul,"[101] establishing an irreconcilable divide between flesh and spirit. As a consequence, the Hellenic heroic culture assimilated a new cult, a spirituality that, as it was "alien in origin, alien to the earlier spirit of Hellenism, and always working in the shadow . . . must be reckoned as one of the forces that prepared the way for the inauguration of a new era and a new faith."[102]

Platonism led to the birth of Orphism, mystical cults, and transcendental religions, which separated man from his natural roots. During this period the Homeric hero—the herald of Polemos and natural laws—lost his will and freedom, his foundation. The hero's freedom and will were replaced by divine designs, the power of rites, and infernal punishments. Since the rise of metaphysical dualism, the ethics of the agonal and Olympic warrior-hero suffered a blow that condemned him to a period of decline that lasted more than two thousand years.

---

[101] Farnell, *Greek Hero Cults*, 380.
[102] Ibid., 402.

Alfred Bäumler—in accordance with the Nietzschean legacy—believed that dualism, introduced in Greek culture by Plato, inaugurated a thousand-year-old madness that drove the Western man down a path that would eventually fragment him and, as Heidegger would then argue, leave him in a constant state of "oblivion of his Being."

"Plato is a coward in the face of reality, therefore, he takes flight into the ideal" [Nietzsche wrote in the] (*Twilight of the Idols*). Since Plato, philosophers have been characterized by a lack of historical sense; that is to say, a lack of conception of becoming. They look at everything as if it was rigid... they mummify it. This is their "egipticism." Plato has strayed from fundamental Greek instincts, he has succumbed to oriental influences rendering the philosopher an "idolater of concepts," a sort of priest. [Nietzsche wrote]: "I shall set apart, with great respect, the name of Heraclitus...." Heraclitus will always be right that Being is an empty fiction. The "apparent" world is the only one.[103]

According to Jessica Wolfe, it is the concept of the pre-metaphysical Agon and how it is embraced that separates the ancient world from the modern world more than anything else. Understanding the essence of this is the key to making it possible to understand the origins of the West, as well as the causes of its decline. Lungstrum and Sauer, in their comprehensive study of the Agon, described the abyss faced by Nietzsche during his cultural struggle for a return to the original conception:

"I am afraid that we do not understand these things in a sufficiently 'Greek' way," complains Nietzsche in his essay "Homer's Contest" (1872). By this, Nietzsche means modernity's problem with thinking agonistically. Specifically, he

---

[103] Bäumler, *Nietzsche der Philosoph und Politiker*. Translated by Giammarco Simonelli.

refers to the late nineteenth century's unhealthy, "softish" attitude toward competitiveness, contest, strife, creativity, and conflict: in short, toward all phenomena inspired by the Greek *agon*. . . . While most people would not dispute that these are indeed agonistic times, there seems to be a guilt-ridden, taboo-like hesitancy to name the human need to play and fight (and to play-fight) for what it is. . . . If the agon is a biologically determined trait that humans have always shared with predatory-yet-playful animals, can (or should) it ever be totally transcended? What forms of sublimation does it take? How do we re-chart the agonal drive to suit the transformed playing field of human existence amidst high-tech productivity and bureaucracy, and to suit ourselves? Can any pragmatic truth be drawn from agonistic behavior's evolutionary gift of adaptability and hence survival? How can boundaries be established and rules be set to avoid harm being done? To what degree is it ever preferable to allow open creative contest, and in which situations are restrictions necessary? What are the spatiotemporal configurations of the agon in modern and postmodern society?[104]

---

[104] Lungstrum and Sauer, *Agonistics*, 1–3.

DISCORD

As the metaphysical tradition gradually swept away the original sense of heroic values, the good Eris was inevitably separated from the bad Eris. Milton Ortiz, a Spanish philosopher, described the rapid process of dissolution of the heroic warrior code. Since the fifth century BC, and more specifically since the Peloponnesian War, Ortiz observed that Greek poetry and culture turned its back on the genuinely polemological heroic tradition in order to associate the heroic dimension exclusively with the destructive aspect. At that time, the war portrayed in the poems of Thucydides "becomes the playground for a human fauna capable of all kinds of vile deeds, stratagems and countless injustices."[105] In the plays of Euripides, the *arete* or virtue of the warrior disappears, becoming instead the root of all social calamities. The Trojan War ceases to be an educational poem and the fruit of cultural pride. "The Athens of the late fifth century BC was a reflection in the shattered mirror of the glory of Troy."[106] In poems and plays, war is described as an ignoble act, a principle of destruction, something that was never rejected by the Greek culture but was placed next to heroism, heroic virtue, and human fulfillment as the ultimate sacrifice for the community.

In this way, the heroic value was demystified and replaced by a less hierarchical approach to the practice of war. Thus, the culture of honor was transformed into an immoral lie supported by cowardice disguised as virtue.[107]

---

[105] Ortíz Escobar, "Pólemos." Translated by Giammarco Simonelli.
[106] Ibid.
[107] Ibid.

So too did Aristophanes in his play *Peace*, in which he perfected the dualistic concept of Polemos. Distant from the figure of father, creator, and preserver of all things, the Polemos of the fifth century BC was merely the personification of destruction and death. In Aristophanes' play, the god Hermes warns that Polemos has captured the goddess of peace Irene. With this, the evil Polemos lets loose his wicked horde, bringing conflict and suffering to the Greek cities. Polemos' mortar and pestle were portrayed as the tools used by the god of war to crush Greek civilization. In a true transvaluation of values, Aristophanes' work ends its story with the Greek citizens rescuing Irene from the pit into which she had been relegated by Polemos, thus restoring peace and justice in the world.

The triumph of the negative and dualistic view of heroism coincided with the decay of Greek culture. The culture that inherited the Greek tradition, the Roman Empire, received an incomplete legacy that lacked the ontological depth needed to understand the concept of Polemos as it was originally conceived. Brian Breed, a Doctor of Philosophy at the University of Massachusetts, explains that in the Roman cultural world the goddess Discordia—the Latin equivalent of Eris—began to acquire an almost exclusively negative connotation. Even Lucan, the Cordovan poet of the first century AD, asserted that the conflict which is intrinsic to nature (*discordia natura*) was heinous and abnormal, a view that would be later expanded by the Cathars and Gnostics during the Middle Ages. Virgil, the author of *The Aeneid*, in a rather ambiguous manner blamed Discordia for the onset of political conflicts and the civil war (*discordia fratum*).

The negative characterization of Discordia in Roman culture was not limited to the destructive aspect of Polemos. The Agon and the civil and athletic competition, losing their polemological essence, devolved into cultural expressions that had nothing in common with their Greek predecessor:

In Greece, sport was primarily competition, Agon, and was not understood as a sporting event for mere amusement. On the contrary, classical Rome experienced sport as a show and, even though the Roman *ludi* acquired over time an increasingly ceremonious character, the spirit of entertainment and exhibition always prevailed.[108]

The process of dissolution of Polemos intensified with the advent of Christian culture in the Middle Ages. According to Francisco Castilla Urbano, it was Erasmus of Rotterdam, the humanist of the sixteenth century, who established a distinct line of demarcation between Christian cultural ethics and heroic ethics. Erasmus rejected any philosophical exploration of conflict, especially that of the ancient Greeks. Erasmus declared that waging war "is not the mark of Christian men,"[109] whether it be holy or just. In Erasmus' view, every type of confrontation or competition was the opposite of love and concord, concepts which were of much higher value according to the ethical standards of Christianity.

The new ideas introduced by the medieval thinkers, scholastics, and humanists marked a total re-evaluation of the concept of life as a struggle. As a result, even the warrior and military tradition—which is always the last possible stronghold for Polemos—was drastically reformulated. The historian Richard W. Kaeuper, in his study of military ethics of chivalry, explains that medieval authors engaged in serious debates over how to harmonize the ideal of transcendental life with warriors' needs. Medieval philosophers openly declared the incompatibility of heroic ethics with Christian ethics, which led to tension between the Greco-Latin warrior code and the Christian religious code. According to Kaeuper, the medieval warrior code tried to relieve this ideological tension—that at a certain moment inhibited drastically the military power of the West which was confronting the Muslim polemological culture—by acknowledging a duality of concepts and values which established that, while in the transcendent world there was only peace and immobility, the life of man on earth was an unavoidable struggle (*Militia est vita hominis super terram*). Because of this, warriors who engaged in combat had to confess and repent for their involvement

---

[108] Monroy Antón, *Historia del Deporte*. Translated by Giammarco Simonelli.
[109] Castilla Urbano, "Concordia y Discordia." Translated by Giammarco Simonelli.

in fighting and for the destruction of human lives once the conflict was over. Chivalry was understood at that time almost as an act of penitence, a way to atone and suffer. The warrior archetype adopted as its foundation the imitation of Christ (*Christus-miles*). In the Middle Ages, heroism became a path to asceticism.[110]

The Christian humanism of Thomas More, Erasmus of Rotterdam, and other medieval thinkers, succeeded in modeling a new warrior code that was ultimately the antithesis of the polemological ethic. The new code was based on rather static and anti-dynamic archetypes. The new hero did not allow himself to lose control because of anger and passion—feelings that were common in the Homeric heroic tradition—but quite the opposite. Composure and a restrained temper were seen as the highest of moral values. The Christian warrior avoided confrontation and the use of force. According to Kaeuper, the humanist Thomas More engaged enthusiastically in the denigration the Greek heroic ethic, condemning the epic poems of war and the heroic archetypes of antiquity. In his work *Utopia*, war was labeled as an activity for beasts. The code of honor described in his book ruled out heroic actions and praised instead every method of avoiding conflict. If conflict was inevitable, it had to be swift and free of any warrior idealism, glorification of leaders, and heroic will.

---

[110] See Kaeuper, *Holy Warriors.*

THE STRONG GODS

Nevertheless, the original conception of Polemos was kept faintly alive and unchanged, thus allowing it to reach the Renaissance and Modernity. Marcus Manilius, a Roman poet of the first century AD, believed that Discordia allowed for harmony and stability, represented as the struggle between conflicting forces. According to Manilius, Discordia was the one who created the world (*discordia semina*). The tradition according to which Polemos was the essence of nature also echoed in medieval authors such as Machiavelli, and even in the theories of St. Thomas Aquinas who wrote about just or holy wars. The same concepts were embraced by the medieval philosopher Nicholas of Cusa, who attributed to discord a positive nature, considering it beneficial and inherently creative.

Perhaps the most eminent proponent of the value of conflict was Giordano Bruno, philosopher and scientist of the sixteenth century. Bruno believed that the only way for entities to achieve individuality was through the discord of the opposites. Hence, he considered the opposites that resulted from conflict to be an integral part of the harmony of the universe. Diana María Murguía Monsalvo, professor at the University of Navarra, observes that Bruno turned to Heraclitus to seek support for his theories, which were based on the observation of nature and the stars. In other words, the interest of Bruno toward Heraclitus was aimed at recovering his ideas in order to corroborate his own observations. This was the ancient philosophy of nature as unity, a non-dualistic universe where the "Whole" (God) was the same as the "multiple" (men and nature), a plurality that emerged from and was rooted in conflict. In this worldview, as Murguía claims, "opposition generates concord."[111] It gives motion to the cosmos, to the becoming and life in a universe where, according to Bruno, "in order to realize concord in discord, the principle of all things must be able to include in itself all the opposites and must be able to generate them."[112] Murguía believes that "neither Heraclitus nor Bruno eliminate or silence the existence of opposition but, on the contrary, they affirm and ratify the existence of contrast, of disparity, for it is precisely contrast that leads to the exaltation of unity and concord."[113] Thus, harmony is not the suppression of opposition.

The Heraclitean vision of the world that permeated Giordano Bruno's thought was at the root of his revolutionary concepts in physics and cosmology. Tragically, these ideas led him to face the censure of the Christian church and, after several controversies and trials that declared him heretical, he was excommunicated and later condemned to die at the stake along with all his writings.

But even if in the European West the concept of life as a struggle was in decline, small traces of Indo-European culture persisted until the tenth century, protected from dualism and the moral polemics that threatened heroic ethics and polemological ideas. The Viking culture, which flourished from the eight to the eleventh centuries AD, preserved, thanks to an abundance of poetry and written prose, a widespread conception of life as a struggle.

No other polemological literary corpus is as extensive as that of the Icelandic Vikings. Obviously, it did not reach the philosophical and scientific depth as did that of Greece and the rest of the West, but it retained a rather more genuine heroic ethic, in which life as a struggle was accepted in its good and bad aspects as a natural principle. And, while in the medieval West was flourishing the poetry of "Courtly Love" or the Arthurian literary cycle of Celtic-Christian origin known as "Matter of Britain," the Scandinavian writers of poetry and prose were not concerned with anything but heroic songs, struggles for conquest, and the honor of combat.

---

[111] Murguía, "Giordano Bruno y la recuperación." Translated by Giammarco Simonelli.
[112] Ibid.
[113] Ibid.

The main source for this polemological culture is the poem of the Scandinavian gods and heroes, known as the *Poetic Edda*, the most complete source on Norse mythology in existence, a collection of stories probably dating from AD 800 to 1100. Also of interest are the mythological stories written by Snorri Sturlson known as the prose *Edda* (which covers themes that differ from its poetic homonym), a manuscript dating from around 1200; as well as the poetry of the Scalds, warrior poets of the medieval Norse courts. Lastly, the Icelandic sagas, which narrate the deeds of kings and warlords, are likewise a source of knowledge about this heroic and polemological culture.

During the ninth century, when Vikings from Sweden, Norway, Denmark, and the colonies of the British Isles conquered Iceland and settled there, events and feats unfolded that would later constitute hundreds of sagas and poems: the formation of kingdoms, struggles and battles for power, love, and revenge. These stories, written only later during the thirteenth, fourteenth, and even in the fifteenth centuries, narrated the adventures of heroes such as Ragnar Lodbrok and his sons, Erik Thorvaldsson, Leif Erikson, the Völsung family, Sigi, Sigmund, Sigurd the dragon slayer, Brunhilda, Gudrun, and so forth, depicting a culture where heroism was related to the constant struggle for existence, the will to power, and the pursuit of new frontiers. To the Vikings, fury was a virtue, and the initiation into the elite of the "Bear" warriors (*Berserkers*) or the "Wolf" warriors (*Ulf-hednar*) who exemplified it was something desired and sought after. The ultimate archetype of the Viking culture was the *Rekkr* (Warrior); but it was not the mere peasant who became a soldier, but the man possessed by the Odinic force of struggle and victory. In the Norse sagas, epic battles were blended with natural magic, giants, elves, and mythological dwarfs, as well as with the continuous interventions of the Norse gods who had an exceptionally warmongering nature. Struggle in the Viking sagas was sought after by the protagonists as a way of gaining prestige and honor. All the main characters were both male and female warriors who followed the Norse religion and its heroic commandments that ordered them to fight against enemies and monstrous beings, so that, at the time of their inevitable death in battle, they would be chosen as dwellers of paradise, the Valhalla, the hall that Odin reserved for the warriors to spend eternity in fighting until the twilight of the gods. Even though the culture of the Vikings sought to avoid war and destruction, conflict was considered natural and a part of life, a universal order not to be condemned but to be faced and embraced as a heroic path to self-fulfillment.

Although many of these sagas were written during the Christian period in Scandinavia, there is no convincing evidence that the Viking polemological culture was altered in order to Christianize these stories, which were written along traditional narratives. A different matter is the phenomenon that these sagas ended up being absorbed and integrated into the epic cycles of medieval chivalry, becoming Christianized and losing their original *ethos*. The most notable case is the *Volsunga Saga*—a tale from 1270 but based on the stories of the heroes of the Volsunga family described in the *Poetic Edda*—which then became the foundation of the *Song of the Nibelungs*, a work written in Christian medieval Germany. According to Jesús Pérez García, professor at the University of Valladolid, this heroic poem contains a strong criticism of the consequences of conflict. This is the great difference between the Western literary heroic cycle—the heroic epic and the songs of deeds—and the Viking sagas. The former certainly told of battles and heroes, but conflict was thought of as a calamity, as a fatality caused by worldly sin. In Western sagas, nothing good came out of conflict and the heroes were doomed to their fate, one that would plunge them into tragedy. In the Viking sagas, prior to the total infiltration of Christian culture, conflict was a path to the gods, an opportunity to reach the highest form of the soul, a characteristic of the natural order from which man could not shy away without losing his essence.

With the complete Christianization of Scandinavia, the taste for sagas did not cease, although the themes changed drastically. Many tales have episodes where their characters convert to Christianity or are definitely Christian, such as the sagas of the Nordic saints. The archetypal models of these sagas are similar to those of the pagan era, but their contents were adapted to the new anti-polemological morality.

According to Jacob Burckhardt, struggle and the agonal principle appeared again unexpectedly in intellectual and philosophical debates in the Europe of the Renaissance. During this period of re-evaluation of Greek values, the most distinguished thinkers began to meditate on the essence of and importance given by the ancient Greeks to the concept of struggle, to Polemos, Eris and the Agon, breaking down the ancient classical texts in an attempt to establish or reject any possible ties with Christian culture. Jessica Wolfe believes that, despite the tendency of Christian humanism during the Renaissance to reject struggle as a positive value in human beings, authors such as Erasmus of Rotterdam, Philip Melanchthon, John Milton, and Thomas Hobbes could not avoid acknowledging the positive aspects that the principle of Polemos could provide to a culture that was renewing itself and in search of new foundations.[114] Erasmus quoted in his works long Homeric passages in which strife was presented as something natural and wondered about the meaning that this agonal value could have had for the Greeks. In the meantime, Baldassare Castiglione and Lodovico Dolce understood *The Odyssey* as a poem that portrayed struggle in its positive, creative, and praiseworthy aspect. To these thinkers, *The Iliad*, which is also referred to as the poem of strength, became instead the archetype of struggle, but still in its warlike and destructive aspect. Odysseus and Achilles were also interpreted as soldiers of Christ and *The Iliad* was understood in some circles as an allegory of the Bible's message. Renaissance philosophers sought ways of understanding the principle of *concordia discors*, the harmony and beauty that came from struggle. Eris was again understood as a multifaceted figure—the cause of the Trojan War, but also of joyful and beautiful events such as the marriage of Peleus and Thetis.

Gradually, the intellectuals of the Renaissance began to recognize struggle and combat as forces that generated vitality, advancement, and ultimately harmony. Words such as *Ponos* (goddess of hardship), *Athlos* (goddess of competition), *Neikos* (goddess of quarrel), *Zelus* (goddess of dedication and zeal), and *Maché* (personification of battle), ceased to bear the negative character that the Christian

---

[114] See Wolfe, *Homer and the Question.*

context had given them for centuries, and were instead considered as typical characteristics of human nature. Erasmus of Rotterdam, for instance, saw the usefulness of disputes with friends in competitive conversation (*verbis certant*) as a quality worth cultivating and whose essence in no way differed from physical struggle. And although these authors strived to find the boundaries between good and bad struggle, the studies of the pre-Socratic philosophers only confirmed the non-dualistic character of struggle.

In the middle of the nineteenth century, the Scottish writer Thomas Carlyle coined the term "Hero-Worship." He was attempting to reclaim the warrior spirit, lost in a society of bourgeois values. But it was precisely the lack of a tradition of heroic values that led him to create the figure of a hero that would be adaptable and suitable to the culture of his century. This new heroic ethic included strong doses of Western humanism, although carrying with it all the ambiguities of medieval speculations. The category of heroes inaugurated by Carlyle included priests, poets, and heads of state, among others. Despite the fact that Carlyle tried to save the modern world from the egalitarian lack of exceptional men, his work ended up becoming an extremely distorted representation of the heroic type.

Nevertheless, Carlyle's attempt presented itself as a roadmap for a return to the original conception of Polemos. The idea of opposing the bourgeois spirit of capitalist liberalism with a heroic ethic suggested a political plan of action that transcended the intellectual meditation relegated to the field of classical studies. But it would not be until the arrival of Nietzsche that Polemos and the Agon would be revalued from a genuinely cultural and revolutionary perspective, presenting themselves as a model for a new cultural beginning.

The path to the restoration of Polemos would be a gradual reversal of its path to dissolution. If Polemos was a cultural concept that initially symbolized justice, creation, and natural law, Western dualism had transformed it into the principle of death and destruction. It was from this negative principle that its positive evaluation emerged again.

The first efforts to meditate on the true meaning of Polemos were made after the Great War. Because of this event, many individuals lived life as a struggle, making a timid—due to the cultural censorship imposed upon it—revaluation possible. Gradually, that ancient nature of man, which was unveiled again in a terrible and cruel way, spread to civilian life, giving Polemos its ancient agonal and creative role back.

But the final impulse for the resurrection of Polemos came through politics. The anti-liberal movements of the mid-twentieth century, such as European and American revolutionary nationalism, as well as Fascism, National Socialism, Sorelian Socialism, or even Marxism, became those in charge of embracing polemological tradition, reacting with a heroic ethic based on the problems caused by the liberal culture of the West.

. . .

Today, "agony" is a term used to define the slow and desperate throes before death, but in the time of the ancient Greeks referred to the process related to the struggle, the Agon. Agony is to endure the struggle, to engage in dangerous situations. The agony of Polemos is, therefore, the struggle of a natural principle regulated by the human spirit which seeks to maintain a balanced relationship between nature and culture. Polemos, the Agon, and the two Eris have not been wiped out of the world, but have been replaced for the time being by other cultural foundations. The anti-polemological present can very well pave the way for a Faustian modernity, where once again the positive aspects of conflict would serve to lay the foundations for a culture rich in material and spiritual creations, preserving a close and healthy bond with the natural order and relieving the dualistic tensions that torture and mortify the man of today.

This "remembrance of being" as the basis for a new modernity was the goal of the Heideggerian polemology, a philosophical project based on the original concept of confrontation, the only one radical enough to force a new cultural and ontological beginning. The spirit of Polemos, however, does not carry with it the reversal of processes such as the globalization of technologies and the cultural contact between the different peoples, ethnicities, and nations of the world. On the contrary, it allows for this close connection from the perspective of difference and true multiculturalism, in which diversity or cultural *panta* is truly respected. Despite the initial strength of the globalist project, its cracks are steadily becoming more and more noticeable. What the American theologian R.R. Reno refers to as "the return of the strong gods" is precisely the sign of the weakening of the myths of liberalism—the empire of the weak gods—and the more and more energetic signs of the return of the archetypes of heroic life.

The polemological tradition regarded Polemos as the father of all things because, for plurality to exist, difference had to exist, and this was only possible through conflict. This occurs not only through the negative connotation of conflict, but also in the situation of standing face to face as sovereign entities. It is for this reason that Polemos is the father of "nonconflictual" human experiences too. For instance, Polemos is the father of love since love needs two opposing entities that are attracted to each other but that do not merge into one. In the same way, Polemos is the father of compassion since it requires an individual to have the ability to feel the suffering of someone else. Polemos is also the father of tolerance, as tolerance requires respect between two individuals whose opinions are opposed to each other. Polemos is the father of all intellectual and sentimental experiences because these all need the interaction with an "other." But it is the experiences which accentuate differences through conflict that play the most important role, in providing an identity through the primordial confrontation. For this reason, cultures with a strong warrior and agonal character are the most faithful to Polemos.

The return of the strong gods, the return of the polemological being, would result in nothing more than the return of man and his culture to their natural path of evolution, the one which has been followed since the dawn of civilization.

BIBLIOGRAPHY

Bauman, Zygmunt. *Liquid Modernity*. Polity, 2000.

Bäumler, Alfred. *Nietzsche der Philosoph und Politiker*. Reclam, 1934.

de Benoist, Alain. "Ni fraîche ni joyeuse." *Éléments* 41 (March 1982): 27-35.

van den Berghe, Pierre L. *The Ethnic Phenomenon*. Westport: Praeger Publishers, 1987.

Bousquet, François. *"Putain" de Saint Foucault: Archéologie d'un fétiche*. Pierre-Guillaume de Roux Editions, 2015.

Burckhardt, Jacob. *The Civilization of the Renaissance in Italy*. Translated by S.G.C. Middlemore. Penguin Publishing Group, 1990.

Burckhardt, Jacob. *The Greeks and Greek Civilization*. Translated by Sheila Stern. New York: St. Martin's Griffin, 1998.

Burnet, John. "Herakleitos of Ephesos." In *Early Greek Philosophy*, by John Burnet, 130–168. London: Adam & Charles Black, 1920.

Caballero, Ernesto Giménez. "Séneca o los fundamentos estoicos del fascismo." January 25, 1934. https://www.filosofia.org/hem/193/fes/fe0408.htm.

Castilla Urbano, Francisco. "Concordia y Discordia en el Renacimiento: El Pensamiento Sobre la Guerra en la Primera Mitad del Siglo XVI / Concord and Discord in the Renaissance: Thinking about the War in the First Half of the Sixteenth Century." *Araucaria* 16, no. 32 (2014). https://revistascientificas.us.es/index.php/araucaria/article/view/794/754.

Cleary, Collin. "Heidegger Against the Traditionalists." *Counter- Currents*, December 11, 2020. https://counter-currents.com/2020/12/heidegger-against-the-traditionalists-part-one/.

Darwin, Charles. *The Origin of Species by Means of Natural Selection of the Preservation of Favoured Races in the Struggle for Life*. Signet Classics, 1958.

Dawkins, Richard. *The Selfish Gene*. Oxford: Oxford University Press, 1989.

Derrida, Jacques. "Heidegger's Ear: Philopolemology (Geschlecht IV)." In *Reading Heidegger: Commemorations*, ed. John Sallis, trans. John P. Leavey, Studies in Continental Thought, 163–218. Bloomington: Indiana University Press, 1993.

Farnell, Lewis Richard. *Greek Hero Cults and Ideas of Immortality*. Oxford: Clarendon Press, 1921.

Fichte, Johann Gottlieb. *Addresses to the German Nation*. Edited by Gregory Moore. Cambridge University Press, 2008.

Fichte, Johann Gottlieb. *Gesamtausgabe*. Edited by Reinhard Lauth, Hans Jacob, and Hans Gliwitzky. Stuttgart-Bad Cannstatt: Friedrich Frommann Verlag, 1962.

Fichte, Johann Gottlieb. *Sämmtliche Werke*. Edited by Immanuel Hermann Fichte. Berlin: Veit und Comp., 1845.

Fried, Gregory. *Heidegger's Polemos*. USA: Yale University Press, 2000.

Gagnon, Jennifer Marie. "Agonistic Politics, Contest, and the *Oresteia*." PhD diss., University of Minnesota, 2012.

Han, Byung-Chul. *The Transparency Society*. Stanford Briefs, 2015.

Hesiod. *Hesiod, the Homeric Hymns and Homerica – Works and Days*. Translated by Hugh G. Evelyn-White. New York: G. P. Putnam's Sons, 1920.

Heidegger, Martin. *Anmerkungen I-V: Schwarze Hefte 1942–1948*. Vittorio Klosterman, 2015.

Heidegger, Martin. *Being and Truth*. Translated by Gregory Fried and Richard Polt. Bloomington: Indiana University Press, 2010.

Heidegger, Martin. *Heraclitus: The Inception of Occidental Thinking and Logic: Heraclitus's Doctrine of the Logos*. Translated by Julia Goesser Assaiante and S. Montgomery Ewegen. Bloomsbury Academic, 2015.

Heidegger, Martin. *Introduction to Metaphysics*. Translated by Gregory Fried and Richard Polt. New Haven: Yale University Press, 2000.

Heidegger, Martin. *Nature, History, State: 1933–1934*. Translated and edited by Gregory Fried and Richard Polt. Bloomsbury Academic, 2013.

Heidegger, Martin. *On Hegel's Philosophy of Right: The 1934–35 Seminar and Interpretive Essays*. Translated by Andrew J. Mitchell. New York: Bloomsbury Publishing, 2014.

Heidegger, Martin. "The Origin of the Work of Art." In *Off the Beaten Track*, translated and edited by Julian Young and Kenneth Haines, 1–56. Cambridge University Press, 2002.

Heidegger, Martin. *Ponderings VII-XI: Black Notebooks 1938–1939*. Translated by Richard Rojcewicz. Bloomington: Indiana University Press, 2017.

Jameson, Fredric. *Postmodernism, or, The Cultural Logic of Late Capitalism*. Durham: Duke University Press, 1991.

Jünger, Ernst. *Der Kampf als inneres Erlebnis*. Berlin, E. S. Mittler & Sohn, 1926.

Kaeuper, Richard W. *Holy Warriors: The Religious Ideology of Chivalry*. Philadelphia: University of Pennsylvania Press, 2009.

Lindberg, Tod. *The Heroic Heart: Greatness Ancient and Modern*. Encounter Books, 2015.

Lungstrum, Janet and Elizabeth Sauer, eds. *Agonistics: Areas of Creative Contest*. State University of New York Press, 1997.

de Mahieu, Jacques. *La naturaleza del hombre: Antropología filosófica del ser humano*. Ediciones Fides, S.L., 2020.

Marinetti, Filippo Tommaso. "Manifesto of Futurism." Le Figaro, 1909. Translated and available at https://useum.org/Futurism/Manifesto-of-Futurism.

McDonald, Melissa M., Carlos David Navarrete, and Mark Van Vugt. "Evolution and the psychology of intergroup conflict: The male warrior hypothesis." *Philosophical Transactions of the Royal Society B* 367 (March 2012): 670–679. https://doi.org/10.1098/rstb.2011.0301.

Monroy Antón, Antonio J. *Historia del Deporte: De la Prehistoria al Renacimiento*. Editorial Wanceulen, SL, 2009.

Morris, Desmond. *The Naked Ape: A Zoologist's Study of the Human Animal*. New York: Dell Publishing, 1967.

Murguía Monsalvo, Diana Maria. "Giordano Bruno y la recuperación de la propuesta heraclítea." *Thémata Revista De Filosofía*, no. 54 (December 2016): 33–52. https://doi.org/10.12795/themata.2016.i54.02.

Mussolini, Benito. *Opera Omnia*. Florence: La Fenice, 1958.

Mussolini, Benito. "Prime basi dello Stato corporativo." Translated. December, 20, 1923. http://www.adamoli.org/benito-mussolini/pag0227-01.htm

Mussolini, Benito. "Speech in Trieste, September 20, 1920." Translated. Biblioteca Fascista, March 3, 2012. https://bibliotecafascista.blogspot.com/2012/03/speech-in-trieste-september-20-1920.html.

Mussolini, Benito. "Trenchocracy." *Il Popolo d'Italia*, December 15, 1917. Translated. Biblioteca Fascista, March 7, 2012. http://bibliotecafascista.blogspot.com/2012/03/trenchocracy.html.

Nietzsche, Friedrich. *Ecce Homo: How To Become What You Are*. Translated by Duncan Large. Oxford: Oxford University Press, 2007.

Nietzsche, Friedrich. *Homer's Contest*. Translated by Christa Davis Acampora. Urbana: North American Nietzsche Society, 1996.

Nietzsche, Friedrich. *Philosophy in the Tragic Age of the Greeks*. Translated by Marianne Cowan. Washington: Regnery Publishing, Inc., 1962.

Nietzsche, Friedrich. *The Will to Power*. Translated by Walter Kaufmann and R. J. Hollingdale. New York: Random House, 1967.

Online Etymology Dictionary. "exist (v.)." Last modified May 3, 2020. https://www.etymonline.com/word/exist.

Ortíz Escobar, M. A. "Pólemos: Una visión ético-política del Fenómeno Bélico en la antigua Grecia En La Retórica Griega." *Revista Perseitas* 3, no. 1 (2015): 34–56. https://doi.org/10.21501/23461780.1427.

Pindar. *Olympian Odes, Pythian Odes*. Edited and translated by William H. Race. Cambridge: Harvard University Press, 1997.

Rivera, Jorge Eduardo. *Heraclito, El Esplendente*. Chile: Brickle Publishing, 2006.

Rushton, J. P. "Genetic similarity theory, ethnocentrism, and group selection." In *Indoctrinability, warfare, and ideology: Evolutionary perspectives*, edited by Irenäus Eibl-Eibesfeldt and Frank K. Salter, 369–388. Oxford: Berghahn Books, 1998.

Schmitt, Carl. *The Concept of the Political*. Translated by C. J. Miller. Antelope Hill Publishing, 2020.

Schuback, Marcia Sá Cavalcante and Michael Marder. "Philosophy without Right? Some Notes on Heidegger's Notes for the 1934/35 "Hegel Seminar."" In

Sorel, Georges. *Reflections on Violence*. Edited by Jeremy Jennings. Cambridge: Cambridge University Press, 2004.

Sternhell, Zeev. *The Anti-Enlightenment Tradition*. USA: Yale University, 2010.

Sternhell, Zeev. *The Birth of Fascist Ideology*. Princeton: Princeton University Press, 1994.

Venner, Dominique. "L'homme de guerre et la cite." *Dominique Venner* (blog), January 1, 2011. https://www.dominiquevenner.fr/2011/01/lhomme-de-guerre-et-la-cite/.

Wolfe, Jessica. *Homer and the Question of Strife from Erasmus to Hobbes*. Toronto: University of Toronto Press, 2015.